While I Am in This Life

Dec. '02
For Kim
a favorite niece +
wonderful young woman.
I'm proud to be your aunt.
Isabelle

While I Am in This Life

MEMOIRS:
SELECTED
VIGNETTES

ISABELLE RUBIN LABELLE

SUNFLOWER PRESS NEWTON, MASSACHUSETTS 2001

Printed and bound in the United States of America.

ISBN 0-971-16450-9

Isabelle Rubin LaBelle
130D Seminary Avenue #323 Newton, MA 02466

People say that what we're all seeking is a meaning for life…
I think that what we're really seeking is an experience of being alive, so that our life experiences on the purely physical plane will have resonance within our innermost being and reality, so that we can actually feel the rapture of being alive.

JOSEPH CAMPBELL
Quoted in *The Little Zen Companion*

A Letter to My Readers

Why write down a story of my life? I'm not famous, nor ever will be. Nor have I made an outstanding contribution to the world. But for myself now in my 70s, memories of my past are too sparse. I have come to the point where I want to recapture more of them, jar them loose, bring them back—the memories of a lifetime. In his book, *The Intensive Journal,* Ira Progoff talks about the value of writing down for "loosening the soil," encouraging additional memories to surface. Memories of much of my life have been unavailable to me up until now. I wondered if they were retrievable. And what memories I had have been too one-sidedly negative (the glass half-empty). I want to see if I can re-experience memories of the parts I've paid too little attention to (the glass half-full).

I believe there are worlds to be gained in listening to—really hearing—our own and others' stories. For each story is OUR story. The psychologist Carl Rogers said that the more he thought a problem or an issue was his own particular idiosyncrasy, the more it turned out to be universal.

Another major spur for writing a life story: Each of us has a need to give meaning to our lives. The older we grow the more our need for frequent, fresh reassessments. Writing about my life is part of this process.

Also, I'd like my children to know more about me as a person—what I've lived through. Why? To enrich their lives—and to help them forgive me, perhaps, for where I fell short.

Sometime back, I received in the mail a packet from a brother-in-law, of photostatted articles from Mama's scrapbook and my high school yearbook, The Sargasso. For awhile, I couldn't—wouldn't—look at this stuff. I tossed it in the back of a drawer. Also, a diary that I'd kept sporadically from 1936 when I was eleven to 1938 came to light. It was ridiculously small. Not enough space to write much of anything. Certainly little space for feelings. I tossed it back there too, consigning to Purgatory anyone that would design such a thought- and emotion-constricting book. And it went out of my head that these glints and glimmers of my life were lying there, inert, in the dark of that drawer.

And I continued to moan and whine that I had few memories of my whole lifetime, and that many of those I had were—alas—of loss and longing, of longing and yearning.

Then I started taking a class at Cambridge Adult Education in autobiography writing. We were encouraged by the facilitator to write down small pieces, vignettes, to get ourselves going.

Finally, I ventured to take a peek into the diary and into my high school yearbook. To my surprise—and chagrin—I found that the dark myths I'd stitched together about my life often bore little relationship to what I'd written at the time.

As I began to look at these jottings and memorabilia from the past, I saw that I'd have to revise much of my story. The prism through which I'd been seeing the world was still binding me. And my reluctance to change was gigantic.

Unmasked. My ambivalence about honestly examining what I'd

been decrying for so long and my reluctance to accept truths that did not fit my myth.

For example: looking at my high school yearbook, The Sargasso, after more than a half century—I saw that along with being the "Scholarship Queen" and valedictorian of our graduating class of 347 (which I remembered full well) I was also second in the "All-Round Girl" contest. Now, that shocked me. I hadn't remembered that at all. All I'd remembered was that I'd failed. I hadn't come in first!!! That my sister Lucy had been All-Round girl in her class was the memory that had lived with me for a lifetime. AND when I graduated from social work school forty years later my Master's thesis and commencement address were on the theme of the need to be SPECIAL—to be Number One. (Talk about being stuck)!

So I'm setting down what I've long known and what I'm coming to see, in hope of living the remaining years and moments as richly as possible.

Acknowledgments

Many people helped to bring this project into being. With his class in autobiography at the Cambridge Center for Adult Education, Kendall Dudley started me on this life quest to regain my memories. My staunch friend David Doolittle and my children Melanie and Josh gave me the caring and encouragement all along the way to help me reach this stage in the process. Melanie, an instructional designer, helped me structure the book and coached me through the publishing process. Josh gave technical support in choosing a computer, setting it up and teaching me how to use it, as well as helping me decide crucial issues, such as what to include in the book.

Immensely helpful were numerous instructors—including Julia Thacker of Radcliffe Seminars; Pauline Briere, a faculty member of the pioneering Lasell Retirement Village, where residents are required to continue their education; and Suzanne Pemsler and Robert Stevens of the Harvard Institute for Learning in Retirement—as were the students in their classes. Lucy Wilson and Ann Silverstein gave moral and technical support along the way. My sisters gave me corrective input about historical details, as well as other feedback. Eleanor Brody did invaluable work copy editing and entering the changes to the manuscript. Designer Gwen Frankfeldt created the text and cover design and coordinated the process of transforming the manuscript into a finished book.

To the memory of Mr. Max Gerber who long ago so generously made it possible for me to go to the University of Chicago, a giant "thank you."

Contents

Prologue: Alive-O

For much of my life I went through the motions without letting what happened to me really get to me . . . really affect me. It seemed to me that nothing would stay the same so nothing I did . . . learned . . . would matter. I had to keep starting over, like Sisyphus, the Greek mortal who displeased the gods and for punishment had to roll an immense stone up an immense mountain. When he got to the top it rolled back down and he had to do it all over again. Consequently and paradoxically—to switch metaphors—I skimmed the surface of life like a water bug.

Now, in my later years I try to learn from—among others—my children. Josh and Melanie go into each life experience with gusto and with the expectation and goal of gaining as much out of it as possible. They live with the assumption that every bit of experience and competence expands into a fuller life, that nothing is wasted.

Coming to the last part of my life, I feel an urgency to make sense of the life I've lived and take active charge of my choices of what's still to be. I yearn to connect more with my alive inner self and to disconnect more from the destructive parts that still roil within me and shut me down—anger . . . fear . . . envy . . . envy is probably the worst.

When I was growing up, I didn't face directly the issues of Independence that usually come up forcefully in adolescence and have to be dealt with again and again at the different phases of life's journey. Compliant on the surface, rebellious underneath. Although I gave the appearance and had the persona of someone successful and together, I was merely pretending to be real, to be alive. I felt like a fraud.

Miraculously, I fooled not only myself (to some extent) but others (perhaps). Thus I went through life. I was good at book learning. I managed to connect with financial help (more of that improbable story later) and thus go to college. I then sabotaged myself by living out a destructive admonition of my mother's: "If anything is given to you without your working for it, it will come to no good."

A fierce life—and—death struggle went on within me—the struggle between living out my mother's injunction—and allowing myself to be truly touched by my life's happenings . . . to live mindfully . . . joyfully.

This story is about my struggle to come alive in the course of a lifetime and to come to believe—and act on the belief—that I deserve and can have what I want.

Kokomo, Indiana

Kokomo, Indiana, the town where I was born and raised, took its name from an Indian chief, Kokomoko, whose tribe was displaced as the whites moved west, taking over their hunting grounds. When I was a child, neither Indians nor Jews were welcome in the country club or the burial grounds. We were Russian Jews. When three of our ten siblings died, they each had to be taken to Indianapolis, fifty-two miles south of Kokomo, for burial.

My brother got beaten up on the way home from school by boys for being "Christ's killer." We girls were not beaten up, just tormented and made to feel defective outsiders. One girl from the rich west side of town taunted me: "I'm Barbara D. in disguise," she'd say, holding her hands over her nose. Barbara D. was Jewish and had a Semitic nose.

The town prided itself on being Midwestern America. The Ku Klux Klan was at home there. Once, Klansmen came into Papa's shoe repair shop and invited him to join, apparently not knowing he was a Jew. "Get out," Papa said.

Among the post-card attractions for tourists displayed in the main park were a stuffed, kind of dusty, two-headed calf, the biggest bull in the world (also stuffed and dusty) and the biggest sycamore stump in the world. The smelly stump was hollowed out. You could go inside and sit down on a cement bench inside it, but you didn't feel like sitting there long because of the musty smell of stale urine. The bark was covered with carved initials joined with hearts. Not an inch to spare.

Another of Kokomo's claims to fame was the invention of the automobile by local mechanic Elwood Haynes, who lived down the street a couple of blocks from us. Others have also claimed to be the inventor. Haynes' shop where he tinkered was in a little brick building at the end of our street, Webster Street. On the adjacent corner, his imposing brick mansion sat on a large manicured lawn guarded by two huge, vociferous dogs.

The heart of town was the courthouse square. Towns still had hearts then, before the malls had driven them out. There, people ran into people they knew and stopped to catch up on the news. The courthouse, a big, square building for conducting official business, had at each corner of the marble halls shiny brass spittoons with wide necks for people to spit out their chawin' tobacco. Peoples' aim wasn't always good and there were big blackish, brown-ish smelly wads on the floor in the vicinity of the spittoons.

On one corner of the square was Hook's Drug Store, where they made the best cherry Cokes in town. The counter clerk mixed the cherry syrup—just the right amount—with soda water and added a slice of lemon if you wanted it. The bus station was in front of Hook's.

Cater-cornered across the street was Armstrong Landon, a hardware store where things were kept immaculately clean and orderly and the clerks hastened to help you find something to fix whatever needed fixing.

On another corner was Newman's Drug Store. You could get a

Coke there in a special Coke glass for a nickel, and a ham salad sandwich on the whitest of white bread with two slices of sweet pickle, for a dime, or a hot chocolate that came in a thick tan cup with whipped cream and two cookies—one chocolate and one vanilla—on a lace doily.

Down the block from the Square was Doris' Ice Cream Parlor where we could go, when we had the money, after the Saturday morning movies, for an ice cream cone with lots of sprinkles for a nickel, or a sundae with butterscotch or double chocolate fudge for a dime. Doris had a tight, strained voice and gray streaked hair in a tight bun. But she liked kids. Her parlor was inviting with its black and white checkerboard floor, cool round marble tables and special ice cream parlor chairs.

The LaMode Dress Shop for ladies was on the block next to the Courthouse Square. Sammy Kopelov, the owner, was a nice man. His son Jerry was sweet on me but I didn't know it at the time. Jerry had a funny way about him. He held his head cocked a little to one side and his voice came out slurred. This made him seem odd and different. I was embarrassed because he was one of us—Jewish. With fifteen Jewish families in our town of 35,000, we tried hard to fit in, to be like everyone else.

There was a beauty shop a couple of blocks from the square. Every once in a while Mama and Leanora, my oldest sister, had the luxury of getting their hair "marcelled"—washed and waved—for a dollar.

Through town, in back of the high school, ran a skinny rivulet grandly called the Wabash River that even had a song about it. "On the Banks of the Wabash." We sometimes sat on its bank and dangled our feet while we ate lunch.

We also made good use of another riverbank—the Indian Trail along the creek, on the south side of town near our house. The trail was steep; the little kids couldn't go on it because it was so dangerous. The older kids taught the younger ones how to tell which tree roots were strong enough to hold on to so they didn't go tumbling into the creek below. It was a rite of passage when the older kids finally gave the go-ahead for a younger one to go on the Indian Trail.

There were two movie palaces in town, the Sipe and the Isis. They were decorated with lots of shiny gold. Saturday morning kid shows cost a dime and sometimes they had a piano player for the silent films. There'd be singing while the reels got changed. The words were shown on the screen and a ball bounced along the words. Everybody followed the bouncing ball, singing.

In fact, there was lots of singing in those days. We'd sing in school, first thing in the morning, the national anthem, and in music class (my sister Leanora was the music supervisor and the only music teacher) and at convocations in the assembly hall. Also, we'd sing at home on Sunday nights when we had company, after serving fudge or popcorn or devil's food cake. We'd stand around the piano and sing "The Indian Love Call"—"When I'm calling you . . . oooh . . . oooh . . . oooh . . . oooh . . . oooh . . . oooh . . . oooh" or "I've Been Working on the Railroad" or "Someone's in the Kitchen with Dinah" or "The Man on the Flying Trapeze."

There was often an amateur hour after the Saturday morning movie. Sometimes I entered the contest with an elocution reading such as "A Poor Old Maid" that made fun of old maids or a reading with a dialect that made fun of someone with a foreign accent.

Oh, it was something—that breath-stopping excitement, waiting to see who got the most claps from the audience. Sometimes I won. The prize was often a free Saturday morning movie.

Occasionally we went to a movie that wasn't a special Saturday morning kid show. Once I went with my older sister Lucy. In those days, the movies ran continuously. You could come and go anytime, stay past the beginning and see the whole show again as many times as you wanted to. The movie that day was The Count of Monte Cristo. We came in where he was digging himself out of prison. It was dark and scary. We went out to the cashier to ask for our money back. She wouldn't give it to us. So we went back in and watched the whole show.

The movies were very mysterious to me. I couldn't figure out how it all worked. Once, Gene Autry and his horse were standing near a waterfall. Would there, I wondered, be water splashing if we went behind the picture screen?

Another thing about Kokomo: it was susceptible to tornadoes. One afternoon a black twister came whirling down in our neighborhood. Houses were blown helter-skelter up into treetops. Luckily, our house didn't get hit. One man, a candy salesman, the father of an acquaintance, had boxes and boxes of candy bars in his garage. He was so thankful that his home had been spared he passed out free Milky Ways to everyone he came across.

A catastrophe that struck the town along with much of the rest of the world was the Depression that followed the stock market crash in 1929. Everybody knew who was and who wasn't on "relief" but people tried to hide it and pretend they weren't. They were so ashamed. Our neighborhood had quite a few blue collar workers who were thrown on relief when they lost their factory jobs at Haynes Stellite (steel) and Delco (radio). Our family wasn't on relief and we were proud that Papa had his own shoe repair shop even though business was slow.

Kokomo was in the center of Indiana, north of Indianapolis (the state capital) on U.S. 31. Endless fields of corn, tall silos and red barns were all along the way from Kokomo to Indianapolis, a drive which we made often because my brother Misch (Harris) and sister Leanora were in college there.

Rhyming Burma Shave ads, catchy little couplets strung along the roadside, were fun to read. Typical ones were:

He played a sax
Had no B.O.
But his whiskers
Scratched
So she let him go
Burma Shave.

Does your husband
Misbehave
Grunt and grumble
Rant and rave?
Shoot the brute some
Burma Shave

Don't lose
your head
To gain a minute
You need your head
Your brains are in it
Burma Shave

Huge ads for chewing tobacco were plastered on the sides of the red barns. A doll house that you could walk into was one of the landmarks that told how far along we were. After the doll house came "Mama's house" on the outskirts of Indianapolis—a huge yellow brick mansion set way back from the highway. It had a high gold-tipped gate all around it. Mama pretended it was our house and we'd say, "Shall we stop off home now or go on to Shapiro's delicatessen first?" and we'd pretend we'd decide to go home a little later.

Shapiro's delicatessen was a feast of smells. Papa would get kosher dill pickles from a wooden barrel and small amounts of lox and black wrinkled olives, and machine-sliced corned beef and rye bread with caraway seeds—still warm from the oven.

Then it came time to say goodbye to Misch and Leanora. Papa would brush at his eyes. It was hard to say goodbye.

Driving home, Papa and Mama were in front and we'd be in back. Darkness would come on, and we'd curl around each other, eat slices of the still-warm rye bread and be lulled to sleep by the hum of the motor and the motion of the car.

An exciting event of the year for Kokomo children was the arrival of the Barnum and Bailey 3-ring circus in the spring. School was dismissed so the children could see the parade. The elephants paraded down Main Street, sweetly holding the curled tail of the elephant ahead. The lion paced his cage. Then later, at circus time, came the ballyhoo of the barker: "Step right up, ladies and gentlemen . . . " and there were all the enticing side-shows—the sword swallower, the fire-eater, the fat lady who sat and jiggled herself, the tattooed man, his whole body except his eyes covered with tattoos, the knife-thrower aiming his knives at his lady partner, outlining her. OOOOh! What if he missed? And the trapeze artists in their spangles, the spotlight following them, the drum rolls . . . then their "death defying" leaps and swings and last-second catching each other. And the clown with his funny costume, big shoes and forlorn, painted face. And hot dogs with sauerkraut, pink cotton candy that vanished with a lick of the tongue with barely a trace of taste, and yellow hot-buttered popcorn. The general admission to the circus, the sideshows and the food treats cost a lot; it was hard to choose what we wanted most, how to spend our little bit of money.

My mother and father had drummed into all of us that we were never to come back to live in Kokomo, once we graduated high school and went off to college. They looked down on people who stayed in Kokomo instead of going off to the "big city"—New York or Chicago—"to make something of themselves."

My parents had come over from Russian cities not far from each other—my father, alone, from Brest Litovsk at the age of seventeen, chased from home by his archetypal mean stepmother. My mother came with her family from Byalystock, a city that was sometimes Russian and sometimes Polish, depending on the geopolitical shifting boundaries. Her father was a junkman, buying and selling from a cart. She was twelve and knew how to read and write. They met and married in Kokomo and had ten (seven surviving) children, including two sets of twins. I was next to the last. A set of twins came four years after me. A first set of twins had died and I grew up in the belief that it was because of me. Many years later it came out at a family reunion that Lucy thought it was she who was the culprit who had given the twins whooping cough and was therefore responsible for their deaths.

After a child who'd been born in the hospital died, and after a close call in the hospital for my mother—her life was saved by a gypsy fortune teller—my mother didn't trust hospitals. She gave birth to the rest of us at home, with the help of a neighborhood woman, Mrs. Derringer, who lived down the block. Mrs. Derringer lived in a dark brown house and always wore dark brown sun glasses and dark brown clothes. (I guess she liked the color brown.) According to Millie she was cruel to her daughter who had a baby out of wedlock. Anyhow, she was helpful to my mother with her babies.

My mother and father got their wish for us. Except for my oldest sister Leanora who came back to Kokomo for awhile, to help my folks out during the Depression, none of us came back to Kokomo to live after we'd once lived away.

MAMA

This section presents a portrait of my mother, "Mama," her personality, her appearance, and how she moved through her world. Writing the vignettes in this section was a way for me to come to a better understanding of who she really was.

"99 and 44 Hundredths Percent Pure"

When I begin to describe Mama, the first thing that comes rushing to mind is that she was old, but in fact she was only thirty-two when she gave birth to me. Formal sepia photographs of Mama and Papa shows them when they were young, both beautiful. She had an oval face then, framed with black wavy hair. Later, her face broadened as she put on weight. Her skin stayed smooth and soft and without wrinkles to the end—to the day of her death at seventy-nine in 1973. The skin of her palms was heartbreakingly pure pink, like the delicate ears of white rabbits.

She was of medium height until osteoporosis gradually rounded her back and compressed her frame. Her body, that had borne ten children, was a soft corpulence with pendulous breasts and soft belly. I was always amazed that she had no self consciousness about letting us kids see her in the bathtub. I don't remember that body ever surrounding me in a hug. We all kissed her and Papa when we came into the house and left it, but it was we who kissed them—on the cheek. I don't remember either of them ever kissing me. But Mama did touch her lips to our forehead if one of us was sick and she needed to see if we had a temperature. I imagine she did when

I had typhoid fever; I just don't remember. Her eyes were brown, as were all her ten children's except mine. Mine are blue and were considered big and beautiful when I was young. Mama never wore glasses. Her eyelids had vertical creases which I despised for some reason. Later, similar creases appeared in mine. Her lips were what showed her disapproval. They would go tight and you would try to figure out what you'd done wrong.

On her fleshy legs there was a tangle of angry-looking thick varicose veins and a red ring from the garters that held up her stockings. Her feet had thickened ingrown toenails that got painful and had to be dug out sometimes. (I have them too. So does Melanie.) She always wore special orthopedic shoes called Enna Jetticks.

She took great pride in her appearance. In our young days, we all took a Saturday night or Sunday bath; later, of course, we took a bath every day. Mama always smelled clean—the smell of Ivory soap—"99 and 44 hundredths percent pure." She would wash her face and put on a fresh apron before Papa came home from his shop at six o'clock. Supper was ready for us all to sit down and eat as soon as Papa washed his hands and arms.

Mama loved to buy new clothes. But she always bought what the children needed first. For herself she bought schmates (the Yiddish word for cheap rags). She'd have a dress "laid away" and she'd pay fifty cents a week at the LaMode Dress Shop until it was paid for and she could bring it home.

When I describe her, I feel teary, a compassion I didn't feel when she was alive and for years after her death.

I can't describe the sound of her regular voice, but when she screamed—which she did often—the world got scary.

Mama loved to laugh. She would cross her arms under her breasts and they would jiggle and shake. It was a laugh like none I've ever heard. Mama did love to laugh. I love to laugh too.

Mrs. Ringle's Belly

It was a hot summer day. I was five. Mama and I were out on the porch swing. The swing made its funny squeaking sound. Mrs. Ringle, our neighbor two doors down Webster Street, came out of her house past Buck's garden next door. She was huffing and puffing up the hill. Mama called out "Good Morning" and went to the sidewalk to have a chat. I went too. They were talking grown-up talk about people out of work and such. I wanted to join in, be part of it.

"Aren't you putting on a little weight, Mrs. Ringle?" I asked, in what I thought was a grown-up way. Mrs. Ringle was a bony lady but her stomach was sticking out like a beach ball.

My mother looked "mortified"—a word she used often—and hustled me away. I didn't know what I'd said wrong. It wasn't until later that I learned that words like "pregnant," "cancer," "abortion," "common-law wife" and "child out-of-wedlock" were only supposed to be whispered.

I ran off to the side yard. A fat yellow and black spider lived in a patch of thorny bushes with shiny red berries the shape of mouse droppings. I took a stick and worried the poor thing to death. Its insides went squishing onto the sidewalk. Then I felt horrible. I never told a soul.

Years later, thinking about that little happening, I fantasized that my mother used that occasion to explain to me sweetly what was growing in Mrs. Ringle's belly and we all three—my mother, Mrs. Ringle, and I—had a good laugh. And the big fat yellow and black spider lived happily ever after.

Ham Salad and Pink Palms

Evergood's Grocery Store in Cambridge carries ham salad, a lifelong weakness of mine. Each week I go into Evergood's and purchase a small container of it, determined to make it last a week. But inevitably in one sitting I devour every last morsel of the delicious diced ham laced with sweet pickles, celery and mayonnaise.

The smell of the sweet pickles in the ham salad pulls into memory a scene from my childhood—one of those rare moments when I have my mother all to myself.

Once in a while, Mama took me with her to town. First she did all her errands around the Courthouse Square: light bulbs at Armstrong Landon Hardware on one corner, toothpaste at the giant Hook's Drug Store on another corner, the mortgage at Union Bank and Trust Co. on another, and down the street a block, Kopelov's LaMode Dress Shop where she paid fifty cents on a layaway dress.

Then we got a treat—lunch at Newman's Drug Store. Newman's had five small round tables with marble tops and ice-cream-parlor chairs. I got to choose—grilled cheese and a malted milk or ham salad and malted milk. Either way, it came with two slices of sweet pickle and cost a quarter. Mama ordered a Coke with her sandwich.

It came in a curvy glass with two straws and cost a nickel.

Mr. Newman gave each of us a glass of water and a napkin neatly folded into a triangle and said, "Isn't it a fine day?"

Mr. Newman's son Bob sometimes helped out in the drug store. Bob was short and had a sunny freckled face. Later in high school he went gaga over Dottie Mae Mills. Dottie Mae was pretty and popular and a dancer and lived on the west side of town. Bob and Dottie Mae would later get married and Bob would die in World War II.

Watching Mama hold her sandwich, I noticed once again her pink palms. Her gold wedding ring was shiny bright. It looked tight on her finger.

Sometimes I imagined Mama looking at me lovingly.

Two Dolls

One day, Melanie, then a teenager, and I, walking in Larchmont, passed a shop window that had on display a strikingly beautiful porcelain doll. Enchanted by the doll, I was reminded of an incident from my childhood and told Melanie about it: One day my mother and I were uptown and I saw in a shop window a darling doll. She had such an adorable face and a whole wardrobe of beautiful clothes—including a lovely tan coat with a fur collar. I just simply fell in love with her. She was very expensive of course. I had never played with dolls. I told my mother I knew she was too expensive and I was too old to play with dolls but I loved her so. If I could have her, I wouldn't want anything else for Christmas/Hanukkah or for three birthdays.

Christmas came—ever so slowly as it did in those days. When I opened my presents, there was that darling, adorable, lovable doll.

Many years later my mother sent me the doll, but I was never sure she was the right one. She didn't have her elegant wardrobe and she didn't look the same. She looked bigger and had lots of chips. I always wondered if my mother had sent me the wrong doll, maybe one of Lucy's. Still, I passed her along to Melanie.

Fast forward: to the Christmas/Hanukkah after Melanie and I saw the porcelain doll. On that Christmas morning there was in our house a buzz of anticipation. I was not allowed to come downstairs until I got the O.K. from Melanie and Josh.

Finally, I got the go-ahead. I came downstairs and there sitting on the buffet was the gorgeous porcelain doll; on her lap, the doll from my childhood.

Melanie, seeing how taken I was by the doll in the window, had gone back to the shop and arranged with the owner to make a deposit and pay every week until the doll was paid for.

The Kokomo doll still rests safely in my bedroom dresser drawer. I still wonder sometimes if she's the very same doll I loved so. Is she an impostor . . . a fraud? She seems bigger and not as fine as my memory of her. I do treat her, though, as if she's the real one. The porcelain doll sits on top of my bookcase in the living room. Not a day goes by that I don't pay attention to both of them.

MY FAMILY

I come from a large, Russian-Jewish family in the Midwestern town of Kokomo, Indiana. My mother, father, brother Harris (in college he re-named himself Misch because there were two Harris Kohns in his art class), Leanora (the oldest girl), Millie, Lucy, the twins—Bobbie and Mary—and I lived in a three bedroom, one bathroom house. I grew up close to my parents and siblings, in both physical proximity and shared experience. My relationship with each member of the family had a strong influence on who I grew up to be.

Bloomer Sunday

An early memory—maybe my earliest, certainly significant. I was four or five. It was Sunday and we were going for a drive, to visit my parents' friends, the Yosts, who lived in the country. In those days going for a drive in the car on Sunday afternoon was considered a treat.

I didn't want to wear the outfit my mother wanted me to—a print dress with matching bloomers. I wanted to wear my little pink rayon panties that didn't show.

"Then you can't come with us," my mother said.

"Then fine. I'll stay home," I said.

"You can't," Mama said. "We have no one to leave you with."

So . . . my Father gave me a spanking. AND I had to wear the detested bloomers.

A lesson seemed to be there's no way you can have what you want. Another lesson: defiance doesn't get you anywhere. It's better just to give in. Could it have been such an incident that prompted me to be labeled with the dread word "selfish"? No one in the family, none of my siblings, can remember a particular incident where I was selfish, yet I was so labeled. This reputation was passed down to the next generation, my siblings' children. A recent visit with a niece brought out the definite statement that I was selfish when I was young. Asked if she knew a specific incident, she didn't.

I remember my mother saying proudly, when I was "grown up," that she never remembers my being angry! No wonder. That was too dangerous. It went underground, turned against myself in a lifelong struggle against depression.

It wasn't until late in life that I came to learn that in an environment of emotional deprivation and lack of abundance anything that one person gets is experienced as taking away from someone else.

My unschooled immigrant parents lacked many of the educational advantages of their second-generation immigrant offspring. That was hard for them and for all of us.

Millie

My sister Millie is a tall, statuesque woman. She gives some credit to Miss Martz, her high school Latin teacher. Millie had gained her height early on in high school and of course in those days girls didn't "go out with" boys shorter then they. She was tempted to round her shoulders and try to make herself shorter. Miss Martz, whose false teeth clicked, called Millie into her office one day, sat her down and said, "Mildred Rosella, you are a beautiful, tall, stately person. Carry yourself that way. Always." That little talk made a lasting impression that Millie has carried with her throughout her life. Even in her eighties, she still gets a second look. The way she carries herself one expects to see a beautiful woman. And one does.

Barrel of Beans

Papa and Mama are in the kitchen arguing, their voices bounding up the stairs where Lucy and I are scrunched down, pinned to the banisters, holding our breath, listening.

"Get a barrel of beans, get a barrel of beans," Papa says. That means they've gotten to the part where he has reached the limit of exasperation and frustration with Mama. I don't understand what it means, but it often comes just before the part where Papa threatens to leave or to commit suicide. Will they get to that part this time? I've never figured out, to this day, why, when Papa and Mama quarreled and he'd reached his wit's end, he'd say "get a barrel of beans, get a barrel of beans." Nobody else in the family seems to remember that or know what it meant.

The argument is over money. It's the time of the Great Depression. There are seven of us children surviving—three died of childhood illnesses. I'm next to the twins who are the youngest. Papa works long hard hours every day except Sunday, but he doesn't bring home much money from his shoe repair shop.

They were of the generation of immigrants who wanted their children to assimilate quickly and become 100 percent Americans.

So they spoke no Russian and no Yiddish at home. At the time, it probably did help us, growing up in the Midwest in a small conservative town with only a few Jewish families. But I, for one, later regretted not having the richness of the dual cultures. I also wonder now what it cost them to do that. It wasn't until I went back to school for another Masters in 1980-82 that I learned that this push toward quick assimilation was a pattern impelling immigrants of that time.

My father was a shoe cobbler and never learned to read written English. He could read print. He read the *Kokomo Tribune* diligently. He tried night school but didn't stick with it. He was always so tired when he came home from the shop. Each of us, as we came along, offered to help him learn to read and write, but he was always too tired at the end of the day. He always thought that's what kept him from doing better in life. Papa had an accent; I was embarrassed and ashamed and ashamed of my shame.

Though they quarreled a lot, Papa liked to kiss Mama on the back of her neck or put his arm around her, even with us kids around, and she'd say: "Oh, Jack" and—glancing at us kids—playfully push him away. Many years later when Mama had cancer and was near the end, she told the twins that she didn't love Papa when she married him. She had only wanted to get away from Grandma, whom she hated, but she grew to love him as the years went on, when she saw how he was with the children.

Papa did have a lot of endearing qualities, and he found pleasure in many things. Some of the things Papa loved:

He loved to hear sopranos on the radio. You'd go into his noisy, dirty shoe repair shop and the radio would be tuned to classical music and when a soprano came on, he'd stand there enthralled.

He loved to care for his lemon tree and see it grow and make real lemons.

He loved to have his back scratched. We'd vie to do it.

He loved to come home from the shop in the evening and after supper in the summer time, to water the grass or mow it, sending up that delicious smell of newly mown grass.

He loved his one glass of wine before going to bed. Mama gave him a hard time about it. She was afraid he might become an alcoholic.

He loved to eat. Some of his favorite foods: herring, salty wrinkled black olives, crisp kosher dill pickles that we kept out on our back porch in the "summer kitchen" through the winter. We'd get a little treat once in a while. We'd also have a bushel of apples out there that we picked in the autumn. They gave the porch an apple-y smell.

Papa also loved to eat everything Mama made—the bread pletzels (loaves) she made Friday nights, potato kugel, gefilte fish on the High Holy Days, home-made noodles, her over-done pot roast that suited him just fine, meat loaf, chicken and chicken soup. Mama could make a little food money go a long way toward feeding the family.

He loved to drive us kids over to watch the steel mill at night. He'd park the car and we'd watch the dramatic pouring of the molten steel into sheets of fire. The heat was so intense sometimes the men fainted.

Then we might go to the donut shop and watch donuts being made in a big window. They'd sizzle and sputter in the deep cauldron of fat and get little warts of dough that were especially yummy to eat.

Or he might take us on a hot summer's night to his favorite fruit stand. He would select a watermelon and the owner would "plug" it so Papa could sample it to make sure it tasted good and sweet. We'd take the selected one home and have the luscious red fruit, sitting around our big wood kitchen table.

Papa loved to get Mama to laugh, and when she got going he'd make a funny little grunt to get her started again when the momentum started to die down.

Papa loved America. He wanted nothing to do with the "Old Country." In Russia, the whole family would share one orange; here in America, each person could have one. He never ceased to exclaim how wonderful this country is, that in this country, with education, a person could do anything. He couldn't understand why anyone would want to go to Europe.

Sitting on the front porch swing of a summer's night after supper, and after watering or mowing the lawn, Papa would exclaim gratefully over the fresh air at home, away from downtown, and the delicious water that came from our own well.

Sometimes our next-door-neighbors, Buck and Florence Ousley, would come over and sit on our porch swing and visit. They'd bring over heaps of tomatoes and other vegetables from their big vegetable and flower garden. Also, Buck would bring Papa rabbits he'd shot and fish he'd caught. Buck idolized my father and admired our accomplishing family. The two families lived side-by-side, each raising their children for many years before my mother got over considering them newcomers to the neighborhood. I'm not sure she ever did. Buck and Florence were "factory people." They always called my parents "Mr. and Mrs. Kohn."

Papa took over some of the household chores. He did the laundry. We had a washing machine in the cellar. He'd wring out the clothes one-by-one through rollers. Water ran all over the basement floor and Papa mopped it up. Then the clothes had to be hung on the line. We helped sometimes. The clothes came out stiff.

Another job Papa did: he fixed Sunday night supper—often Aunt Jemima's pancakes with lots of maple syrup. Mama's work on Sundays ended with preparation of the big mid-day dinner. Also,

Papa made breakfast for us kids in the morning. He himself had a raw egg in the morning. He'd prick a hole in the end and tilt back his head and slurp it right down. "Ooooo," we'd say, making faces. He also gave us children hot milk at bed-time. Once I guiltily threw it down the sink when he wasn't looking.

In the morning he'd get up before four A.M. to start up the furnace so the house would be warm for Leanora to practice her piano before school. I felt comforted by the sound of the shovel thwacking on the open mouth of the furnace, knowing Papa was warming up the house for Leanora, for all of us. Seldom in the course of my life have I felt that "all's right with the world" comfort of those early mornings. I was awake and I was asleep. Sleeping, I felt warmth.

Papa didn't want any of us to spend too much time in the shop. He felt we should be doing better things with our time—like studying or practicing.

My brother Harris' teacher at John Herron Art School didn't think much of his future as an artist. He thought Harris should go to work with Papa in the shop. Papa wouldn't hear of it. He wanted a better life for Harris, as for all of their children. I wonder how that teacher's life as an artist has gone. Misch has had wide success and recognition of his pioneering work as a printmaker and had a traveling retrospective of sixty years of his work.

Somehow Papa had always managed to scrape together the money for Harris' costly oil paints though sometimes he had no winter coat. One winter, my sister Millie saved up from her lunch money and bought Papa a coat for Christmas/Hanukkah. Once, he lost ten dollars, a whole day's take. Leanora put ten dollars out in the yard and pretended she found it so he wouldn't feel bad.

Some frequent sayings of Papa's were ". . . as long as you've got your 'helt' " . . . "I wouldn't take a million dollars for any one of you children" . . . and "we love all of you the same," but we all knew who the favorites were, though I don't remember ever talking about it among ourselves. Millie was Papa's favorite among the six girls. And she was considered the family beauty. (Millie and Mama didn't get along.) Of course, Harris being a boy and their only surviving son, was all-time tops. That's just the way it was. I don't remember feeling jealous of Harris. I'm sure, looking back, I couldn't have allowed any such "bad" feelings to reach awareness.

Millie has always been admired and liked by men. Maybe partly because of her early success with Papa, she's "had a way with" men. Men liked her, not just because she was considered beautiful; she made them laugh and feel good and she'd bring into the office cookies she'd made. In her years working in doctors' offices, she'd tell about the other secretaries in the office being jealous of her because of the way the doctors paid her attention.

"Am I pretty"? I once asked Papa. He scrunched up his mouth and shrugged. Maybe he believed as Mama did that you should never give a child a compliment. She might get a "big head," might get "spoiled." "Spoiling" a child was a heavy fear in those days.

I remember one sepia photograph of Papa when he still had a full head of black curly hair, holding one of the children, probably Harris. He's standing in a lake, wearing a fashionable knee-length bathing suit. In the early years mama and papa seemed to do fun things with the children. I haven't come across such photographs of the children who came on the scene later.

Papa and Mama expected us kids to do better than they had. Of course, this assumption about the younger generation has seen a shift in the past few years. People don't necessarily expect to do better financially than their parents. There's much more uncertainty about the future now.

Thinking about it now, it seems strange to be raised to look down on the town you grew up in and on the townspeople who remained there.

Life for Papa and Mama was a relentless struggle over money. They scraped to pay the mortgage, and keep a car—usually a second-hand Plymouth or Chevy. They were always paying off a bank loan at high interest. Insurance was saved each week—fifty cents—in an envelope on top of the upright piano. The insurance man came around to collect. After Papa died in 1963 and then ten years later after Mama died, each of the children inherited one thousand dollars except for Misch. He got more. Each grandchild got one hundred dollars. I put my money toward a brand-new green Dodge Dart, paying cash, which my parents had never in their whole lives been able to do.

Papa wore thick glasses. His weak eyes burned and watered. His fingernails were black and ragged. He had an angry-looking scar on his hand, around his left wrist. His story of that scar was that when he was a boy back in Russia he had an accident (what kind?) and somehow cut off his hand and the doctor sewed it back on. He was working on the motor of a car. Someone turned the motor off. The fan almost completely cut off his hand at the wrist. He held it together and someone took him to the hospital.

When he'd cut himself at the shop, he'd just seal it up with some rubber cement and go on working. It's a wonder he didn't die of blood poisoning.

Papa was good to Grandma, Mama's Mother—better than Mama was. (Mama hated her.) After his Sunday morning bath, he put on a fresh white shirt and went to visit Grandma. He always took some of us kids with him. This got us out from under foot so Mama could prepare the big Sunday dinner that we had in the middle of the day. Usually chicken or pot roast. We liked to go, mostly to be with Papa. He gave Grandma money. She gave each of us kids a dime except for the twins; she gave them a nickel apiece.

Papa called most of the Jews in Kokomo "kikes," that's an insulting word for a Jewish person. Russian Jew that he was, he was anti-Semitic, I realized later. Most of the Jews in Kokomo were better off financially than we were. He felt looked down on. And he was probably jealous. His life-long dream was to escape from being a shoe cobbler. From time to time he tried other ways to make a living. Once he bought a bowling alley but that venture failed dismally and he had to go back to being a shoe cobbler. He had a brother, Arthur, in Hayti, Missouri who was well off but never helped him. When Arthur died, he left Papa not a red cent in his will. This was bitter gall for Papa.

Sacrifice is a word you don't hear much these days. We heard it often when we were growing up. To Papa and Mama their family was their life and they did sacrifice for us kids. And we were never unaware of that and always felt the heavy responsibility to make it up to them—an impossibility of course—by achieving. We did achieve, but at high cost—the cost of a lifetime of unease of feeling whatever we accomplished was not enough.

Papa died at the age of seventy-five. He had smoked three packs of cigarettes a day all his life from the time he was very young until he got lung cancer and died. He always coughed. He knew cigarettes were bad for you. When he was in the hospital, he tried to get everyone in the family who smoked, to stop.

In the funeral eulogy, the Rabbi (who was Millie's daughter Judy's husband) said Papa was a man of great strength. That was a surprising thought to me. I'd always thought of him as weak and led around by the nose by Mama. But maybe he was strong in not combating Mama more than he did. Their relationship was tempestuous enough as it was.

Papa was buried in Kokomo where he had lived out his life. So times had changed. They now allowed Jews to be buried in the town. Progress. After his funeral, we all went to a nearby orchard and picked a barrel of apples. Papa would have loved that.

Papa was a good man, a hard-working man. He believed fiercely in America and in education—that in America anything was possible with education. I still don't know whether he was strong—as the Rabbi said at his funeral—or weak—as I thought at the time. Both, I guess. He certainly did the best he could with his life, given the tough hand he drew.

Grandma

My Grandma—my Mother's Mother—was a tiny old woman with a fuzz of white hair caught in a puffy knot at the back of her neck. She had a weird way of drawing her hand across her toothless, sunken mouth and hairy chin while making a strange clucking sound. She lived in a small, dark, spooky brown house with a big front porch near downtown Kokomo. Aunt Elizabeth ("Lizzy") and Lizzy's son Ted, by her bigamist husband, lived with her, as did Grandpa.

Grandpa was old, sick, and blind. He stayed in a little dark room off the dining room. He finally committed suicide with gas, stuffing rags into the window cracks.

Grandma was glad to see us every Sunday morning when Papa brought some of us kids to visit. She always had on a clean apron. I don't remember my Mother ever visiting Grandma. I wonder now if she went to her funeral. I guess she probably did.

I used to have mixed feelings about going to Grandma's on Sunday mornings. I liked to be with Papa, and Grandma gave me a dime. But I hated that we had to kiss her dry wrinkly cheek when we came and left. I also felt ashamed to be related to her with her poor English and to my Grandpa in that dreary dark little room.

Grandma was to live a long time, ending by insanely hiding feces and dollar bills rolled up into tight pea-sized balls all over that spooky brown house, upstairs and downstairs, on the walls and in every container. Everywhere.

I know absolutely nothing of my Father's parents. They stayed in the "Old Country" when my Father came to America from Russia. Did he ever have any contact with his family after he came over? How did he feel about them?

I am sorry that I know nothing of all this except that while he loved his Mother dearly, his Father's second wife wanted Papa out. So he left Russia and came to America to try to make his way.

When I hear people speak of their Grandparents with love and devotion, as a strong and nurturing influence in their lives, I feel deprived. We missed out on that.

The Fuchsia Door Knob

I'm thirteen.

One of my older sisters says I'm smart but I only have book-learning. Another sister says I have nice shoulders but the black-heads on my nose are awful. Mama says I'm selfish.

But somehow when I look deep into that shiny fuchsia cut-glass doorknob that belongs to my sister Millie, those awful words quit hitting me. I see an Izzy that does have common sense and is pretty and lovable.

How I love that fuchsia doorknob. It's my favorite thing. With all my heart I love that fuchsia doorknob. It's Special. Millie knows I love it. Aunt Marie gave it to Millie: Millie is Aunt Marie's favorite. Millie is a favorite of Papa's too—even though Papa and Mama always say they love all seven of us kids equally. And Papa always says he wouldn't take a million dollars for any one of us. Millie has a fiery temper but she loves to make people laugh. And she loves to make fudge and cookies and other goodies for people.

Millie plays the violin. Mama wants her to be a famous concert violinist. Mama knows what she wants each one of us to be. Mama wants Leanora to be a famous concert pianist.

Since Harris is so set on being an artist, maybe it will be O. K. for Mama if he'll be a famous artist.

Millie has been practicing her violin, standing near the living room register to keep warm and she asks me to run up to Puckett's—that's the corner grocery store—to get a jar of green olives stuffed with red pimentos. She loves to eat them when she takes a break from practicing. This is all long before she went off to college and had a baby her first year there and later ruined her hand in a Mixmaster and was never able to play her violin again.

On the day I'm talking about, she gave me a dime saved from lunch money. I ran to Puckett's. We sucked on the vinegary juice the olives are soaked in and then slowly nibbled the red squiggly squares and the tart green. We could make an olive last a long time.

We were sitting on the living room furnace register, warming our bottoms when Millie said out of the blue, "You can have my fuchsia doorknob." I couldn't believe my ears. For so long I had "coveted" (to use a word from the Bible) that magical fuchsia doorknob. Such a splendid thing it was. Suddenly it was mine.

I felt like skipping.

But then, not long after, once it was mine, a strange thing began to happen. The wondrousness of it fizzled away. Was I doomed, I wondered? Would it forever happen to me my whole life that anything that was mine would turn into being nothing special?

A Hanging Tale

It was 1933, bitter Depression times. My brother Harris was in his first year in art school in Indianapolis, Indiana, his first time away from home. He had rented a room in a boarding house—a fourth floor attic room, a dark, scary cavernous space. To go to the bathroom, he had to go down three flights of pitch-black stairs

His second night there, another young man came to live in the attic.

"What a relief to have company," Harris thought. The fellow was in a work/study program at Antioch. Harris gave him some of his meager supper that he'd brought from the cafeteria where he worked for his meals. The young man looked emaciated and his eyes glinted.

As they were eating, the young man, looking up at the rafters, observed "It would be a good place to hang yourself."

The next night, when Harris came back, the landlady informed him the new roomer was no longer there. He'd hung himself on the attic rafter.

Later that night, when Harris had to go to the bathroom, terror-stricken at the thought of going down those stairs, he urinated out the window. Then he shat into the newspaper that his supper had been in. He didn't know what to do with it. He wrapped it up and threw it out the window.

The next night, when he returned to the boarding house, his belongings were out in the street.

"You're out," the landlady said.

"Why?" he said. "How could she know it was me?" he wondered.

Harris walked to the basement apartment of a new-found friend in his art class and stayed with him that night until he could look for a new room.

BELONGING

As we were a distinct minority in Kokomo, I often felt like an outsider in the town and its society. At the same time, my brother and sisters and I were very accomplished as students, musicians, artists, writers, and dramatists, and this gave us a place of respect within the community. This push-pull of feeling both like an outsider and an integral part of the community was a dynamic I struggled with throughout my childhood.

Encounter at the Creek

The whole neighborhood is down at the creek. People are in the water searching for Carl De Long. He was last seen at the creek hours ago. It's past six o'clock. Past supper time. Darkness is coming on. Before long, they'll have to give up the search.

Suddenly, a stranger to the neighborhood, an old man with a sad, wrinkly face is standing near me in the water. What is he doing? It's hard to see because of the growing dark. He takes something out and rubs it against me. I feel I ought to run away, but I'm surprised and curious. What's that in his hand? He rubs it up against me near the top of my leg.

"Does that feel good?" he says in a soft voice. "It's supposed to feel good." I feel it's wrong to let my curiosity glue me there. Finally, I twist away. My face is burning. I won't be able to tell anyone about what happened. I should have run away right away.

They find Carl. They pull him out of the water and lay him on the sand and take turns pumping him. He doesn't breathe.

It's dark now. Mrs. De Long is screaming.

Crazy About Willy

My high school days seemed like one long yearning. I had a mad crush on Willie Knipe the entire four years. He was extraordinarily handsome—straight aquiline nose. Tall. Dry and droll sense of humor. His locker was right next to mine. But he didn't know I existed—couldn't he hear my heart beating when I was near him? We sat next to each other in the orchestra—shared the same music stand. He was a good flutist and piccolo player and I was not. (I did lots of "faking it" at concerts.)

He was the class president, of course.

I later found out—at our fortieth high school reunion—that all the girls had been crazy about Willie but I was so out of the loop of the "in" west side crowd that I didn't know that.

In fact, when I went to the fortieth high school reunion—the first one I ever went to—I didn't have the—whatever it took—to go before that, I had my sister Millie come with me; I felt so unsure that I would feel comfortable. When we got there, I went right up to Dorothy Hunt—she was the west side girl he finally settled on and married right out of high school, and I said, "Dorothy, the first thing I want to do at this reunion is tell Willie something. Where is he?"

She pointed and I went right over to him and said: "Willie, I want to tell you that all through high school I had a mad crush on you." He whooped and hollered and said, "Izzy, you couldn't have said a nicer thing." And he grabbed me and hugged me. And my sister Millie too. All during the whole reunion when pictures were about to be taken, Willie would say, "Come on over here, Izzy," and he had me stand next to him and he put his arm around me.

Ten years later for the next reunion, the fiftieth, Willie asked me to be one of three after-dinner speakers at the main event at the Kokomo Country Club. My memories of the country club were of us kids scrambling along the Indian Trail next to it, holding onto the tree roots to inch across. We'd be hot and sweaty. When we got to the top, we'd peer over and see people by the swimming pool, cool and collected, having frothy tall drinks. Jews were not welcome in the country club in those days, just as they were not welcome in the cemetery. So all these years later, to finally get into the "sanctorum" of the country club as a featured speaker was something.

People age so differently, physically as well as emotionally. Willie was as gorgeous as ever. Willie's wife, her body now ample, had the same porcelain skin and lovely features as she did in her girlhood. One woman, who had been a cute, adorable girl, lacked the beauty of aging that many older people have. One woman who'd been a plain girl was a handsome woman of the world.

One man seemed to be making a big effort to sit next to me at the dinner. "Were you in Chicago on the South Side in 1945?" he asked. "I thought I saw you when I was driving, but you went into a building and I lost you. I've always wondered, ever since, was it you?" I didn't remember him.

Many people were gone already, some from wars, others from "natural causes." Since Willie and Dorothy had been the main coordinators of the reunions, this one might be the last. Willie had cancer.

I was really glad I'd upped and said what I did at the fortieth while we were both still on this planet.

Papa, young.

Mama, young.

My parents with Harris (later named Misch)

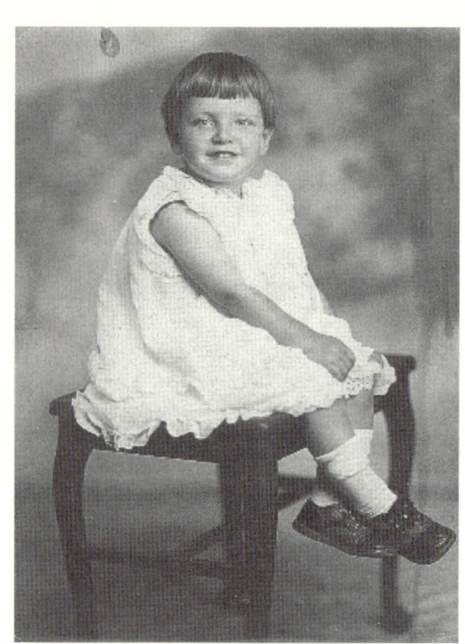

Me

The five of us children (I'm the youngest, in the middle) before the twins came.

Peter Rabbit tableau. Mrs. Baldwin's first-grade class. There's Mr. McGregor, standing in his cabbage patch. There's adorable Billy McCann, my first love, right in the center. There I am sitting up on the left, third rabbit from the right. I had always remembered this scene and recently this photograph came to light. I was so glad to see it. Angelic as we all look, I spit in a boy's ear that year and Mrs. Baldwin sent me out in the hall. Billy did something bad so he'd be out in the hall with me.

To the dearest father in the world.

These little gifts that we give you can't begin to express all the love we have for you, Papa. But we just want you to know that we think you are the sweetest, sincerest, most lovable Dad that ever was.

We all love and admire our "Papa" so much that words can't express it.

Love,
Izzy

A birthday note to Papa.

AUGUST 27

19 I went with Mr. White to camp. We had dinner and supper and campfire I slept all night there

Frid. 19 Didn't win Amateur Contest. Crazy cowboy songs won. The show was good though — (Palace Theater) Might still get bike.

19

AUGUST 28

19 I came home fro
camp this evening
about 15 minutes till
8:00. Camp is near Greer

19 Sat: It was honestly happiest day of
life. We picked out bike. I squeal
asked Papa — he said we'd
a coin. If mine matched his, I
it if not — I didn't. Mine did. I
bike, rode it home. Lucile r

19

Diary entries, 1936.

JUNE 8

1936 I went to the Yard on the way home Della and I stopped at Grandma's who gave us a jar of pickles.

1937

JUNE 9

1936 I took my dancing today. I am getting good in tap but I am not limber enough yet.

1937

Lucy's birthday party. I stood outside the circle. I didn't know I was in the picture.

Confirmation class.

High School portrait.

In the high school yearbook, *The Sargasso,* this photo was captioned: "Second honors in the choice of the All-Round Girl go to Isabelle Kohn, who graduated with an all-A record, and countless credits in attendance, art, dramatics, publications leadership, programs, music, school and civic service, health and religious service. Few girls have been so ready to serve when needed."

Willlie Knipe (middle) and me (on right) next to Willie. I had a crush on Willie all four years of high school.

Kokomo High School. A singer, Jessica Dragonette, visits, gives a performance.

Buggy ride with Mr. Gerber, my sister Mary and a friend.

Papa and Mama, their wedding picture in the background.

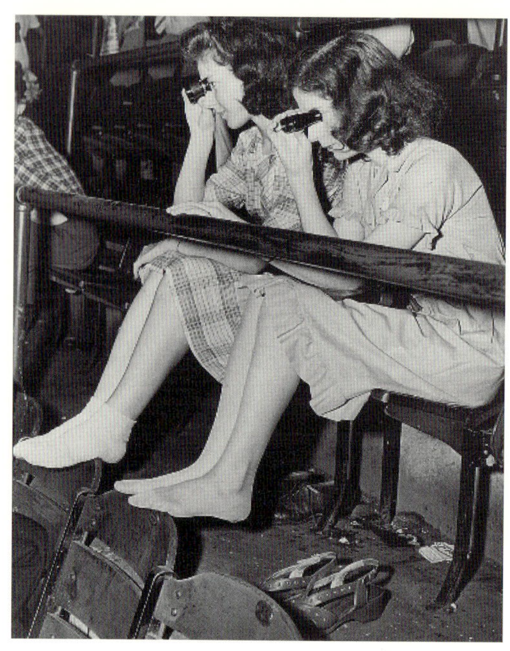

With a friend, attending the Republican nominating convention at the Chicago Stadium, 1942.

Out on a limb and liking it. At the University of Chicago.

At TIME-OUT party, 1949.

Our whole family together, 1956.

Josh, Ray and me.

Melanie and Josh in straw hat.

Vacation:
Jamaica,
West Indies

Josh

Ray and Melanie.

Ray, and Josh and Melanie, with pet guinea pigs.

Melanie dancing.

Melanie in an Easter bunny outfit, with friend.

Melanie at a favorite activity—cooking.

Josh and Melanie, on the back porch of our Larchmont town house.

Josh dangling from a tree, and Melanie.

Three commencements:
Melanie from Brown,
Josh from law school,
myself from Yeshiva.

Josh, Melanie and me at my photography show of Nepal and Indian photographs.

Melanie and Josh share a wildreness trip with their father, Ray.

Josh and Stephanie (later, his wife)

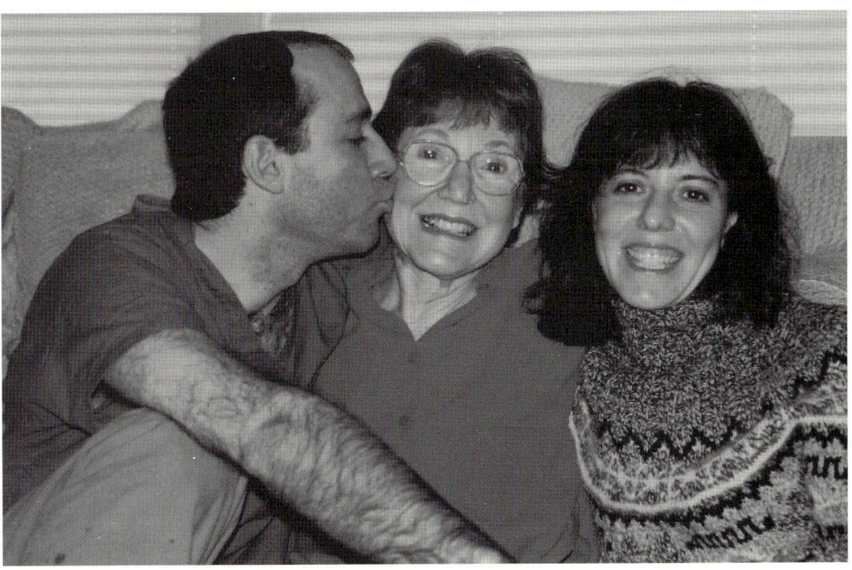

Josh, Melanie and me holidaying in Bend, Oregon, 1996.

The twins,
Mary and
Bobbie.

My first "date" with second husband Robert L. LaBelle, 1985.

Our wedding celebration, 1985.

The six sisters at my wedding.

Thanksgiving. Santa Cruz, California. The original seven siblings at a family reunion. First time we'd all been together since Mama's funeral in 1973.

A WORLD GONE BY

The world I was born to and grew up in doesn't exist anymore. In these stories I try to show what my world looked like and felt like—as a child, a young adult, and a maturing adult—and what was important back then.

Champion Fudge-licker

Alberta Ripberger could make a piece of fudge last the longest of any of us South Webster Street kids. We would each put a sweet brown chunk of fudge on our tongue and slowly, slowly lick it. But when we thought we were surely the winner and champion fudge licker, Alberta would fool us into thinking she'd finished hers. Lo and behold she'd still have a tiny sliver left. So we all went down to defeat once again. Once again, Alberta Ripberger was the champion fudge-licker of South Webster Street.

Scrapbooks; Sunday Night

It's Sunday night. Mama and Papa are entertaining. The house has been thoroughly cleaned and vacuumed and the furniture polished on Friday by sundown—candle-lighting time. Some of us kids have made popcorn and fudge or devil's food cake with dates and nuts. The mixed smells of furniture polish and the mid-day Sunday roast dinner linger in the house.

After the company has sat and visited awhile, Mama asks Leanora to play the piano. Leanora sits down and plays—often Chopin, Mozart, Rachmaninoff or Beethoven. Sometimes De Falla's Fire Dance for a change. The audience claps heartily. My Mother and Father qvell. (Yiddish word: experience intense pleasure.) Then Mama asks Millie to play. Millie tunes up and plays her violin, accompanied by Leanora. The guests again clap long and loudly.

I'd like some of that attention too. Mama asks me to give an elocution reading. The guests call out their favorites. I decide on "A Poor Old Maid." I recite the monologue with the exaggerated gestures and expression I've learned in my elocution lessons. I soak up the applause.

Sometimes if Miriam Klein is among the guests, she'll favor us, after being coaxed, with a rendition of an operatic aria. Miriam Klein used to be an opera singer. She is tightly corseted and has orange-red hair (out of a bottle, my Mother says) in tight little sausage curls. As she warbles, her fat fingers, with their long red nails, clasp each other on the shelf of her bosom and ride up and down dramatically. She's rich and lives on the west side of town, of course.

Mama had wanted to be an opera singer. She never got any training. But she buys music lessons for all of us kids.

Then it's time for the scrapbooks. Mama proudly brings out the current one and puts it on guests' laps open to the most recent *Kokomo Tribune* clippings about recitals and honors we Kohn girls and my brother Harris have won. I sometimes wonder if people really want to read all those clippings. The Sunday night doings feel both comforting and embarrassing. Do people laugh at Mama behind her back for bragging about her kids? I can't imagine now, looking back, that they all necessarily wanted to read about our little triumphs. But maybe the company and the refreshments were enough enticement.

Then we often gather around the piano and sing—often many of the same songs we sang at school.

Mama is ambitious for each of us children, with her heart set on Millie's becoming a famous concert violinist and Leanora becoming a famous concert pianist and Harris becoming a rich and famous artist. All of us kids work hard to please Mama.

What happened to those ambitions of Mama? During the Depression, Leanora, postponing her high ambitions to be a concert pianist, came home to Kokomo and taught music in the public schools. It hurt her voice; she was speaking and singing so much. She finally left Kokomo and moved to Chicago where she got a job as a researcher on Coronet magazine, met and married an artist friend of Harris's and had two children. She played the piano sometimes. She now has Alzheimer's.

After her hand was damaged in the Mixmaster, Millie became active in music clubs of Cincinnati. She has three children, four grandchildren and one great grandchild.

I don't recall Mama's specific early ambitions for Lucy, Bobbie and Mary, but Lucy trained as a nurse, and served as an Army nurse in World War II. After marriage and children, she earned a Doctorate in Psychology and became a psychotherapist.

Bobbie married a man who became a university professor of genetics. She later became a librarian, then an art museum docent, and then an art historian.

Mary married a man who became an academician but an extraordinary maverick, highly recognized and honored. Through the years, Mary became more of an equal partner in their varied wide-ranging joint projects that took them around the world far off beaten paths.

All of us children worked hard to please Mama. But driven to achieve as we were and achieving as we did, we never felt we had done enough.

The Yosts

The Yosts were long-time acquaintances of my parents. They lived in the country outside Kokomo. Sometimes on Sundays we'd take a drive out to visit the Yosts and buy fresh eggs. And sometimes we kids—one at a time—got to go to their farm for a week in the summertime. I don't remember the Yosts ever coming to our house.

There was Frank Yost. He was so handsome. He didn't have a beard and he was brown from the sun and you could see white skin when he rolled up his shirt sleeves. Frank wore bright red suspenders. He had a dimple on his left cheek that showed when he laughed, which he often did. I can see Frank's face and hear his laugh right now, thinking about him. I had a crush on Frank back then. And there was his wife and their daughter Esther. Esther had a twangy-thin voice and was an old maid (probably around twenty-three or twenty-four and not yet "taken"). Later on, she got married and had children.

Mrs. Yost and Esther wore little white starched pleated caps and long skirts down to their ankles and big aprons with a small flower print. Also, there was Mr. Watts, the Grandfather. He had a big barrel-body and wore black suspenders.

The Yosts were very religious Christians—called Mennonites. They had different ways from our family. They said Grace before they ate. They put their palms together and touched their fingers to their chins. As Russian Jews, we didn't say Grace at home. We did there, of course.

They had a large black stove in one corner of their kitchen and a large round table in the center. Mrs. Yost and Esther made breakfast for the men while they were out milking the cows. Then the men came in and pushed up their shirtsleeves and washed their hands in shallow tin pails. I loved to watch the water turn dirt-color.

The Yosts ate big breakfasts—piles of eggs and bacon and cereal and toast and home-fried potatoes and cereal and jam. Sometimes pancakes. It was totally delicious.

They had a party-line telephone. It was black and tall and heavy. There was a part to talk into and a part to hold to your ear. When someone wanted to make a telephone call, they'd crank up the phone. If someone was already talking on the line, they'd have to wait. Sometimes they'd listen in just a little. But if they needed to make a call in a hurry—of course they were seldom in such a rush—they'd just tell the people talking on the line and they'd get off and let them make their call. They all knew each other. They were neighbors.

There were lots of things to do at the Yost's farm. I was allowed to collect the warm eggs from the chickens with Esther. The chickens squawked and scolded and flew about when we took their eggs. There was hay in the barn. It was fun to jump in it. There was a lamb and a little pony cart; Esther pulled me for rides in the meadow. She wasn't too busy to take time out from chores.

The Yosts made their own soap. It takes a lot of boiling in a big black kettle. I helped stir. And they let me help churn the butter. That took a long time too, patiently pushing the pole up and down.

The thing is, with all they had to do, they never seemed to rush. They were always calm. Mrs. Yost didn't get mad at Esther and yell. And they didn't shoo me out of the kitchen so they could get their work done. I could help with chores when I wanted to. And the rest of the time I could just play.

The thing about being at the Yosts was, I didn't have to always be accomplishing something so I'd be mentioned in *The Kokomo Tribune*. I'd get mentioned—and also get a quarter or a box of candy or a handkerchief—for giving elocution readings to entertain the Masonic lodge and other gatherings.

The Yosts didn't keep scrapbooks. At night after supper when the day's chores were done, we'd all sit together in the living room. The light of the kerosene lamps was soft gold. Esther and Mrs. Yost took off their aprons and did needlework and the clock ticked away and made deep bongs on the quarter- hour, half-hour and hour. And the rocking chairs made their comforting sound and the men read. And so did I. One of my favorite books to read there was Hans Brinker and the Silver Skates. It had a bright orange (I love the color orange) cloth cover that felt nicely rough.

Another good thing about being at the Yosts: it was nice to have adults all to myself sometimes, with none of my five sisters getting all the attention. Frank and Mrs. Yost didn't touch much during the day, but there was a feeling of peace and contentment around them. And all the Yosts smiled a lot.

When it was time for bed, at the end of the day, Mrs. Yost and Esther lighted the way up the stairs to bed with the kerosene lamps. I looked at the sky out my window in the summer. The night air was so sweet and heavy—you could practically eat it. And the sky was so velvety black with billions of sparkly stars and the Milky Way was thick and wide and looked like spilled flour. And the sound of the crickets was really loud.

Mr. Max Gerber

Who could have imagined that day when I nervously set out for my appointment with Mr. Gerber that that morning's encounter would give form to the best and the worst directional forces of my life for years to come?

I was sixteen, a senior in high school, thinking about going off to college, wondering how on earth I could manage to pay for it, but never considering the possibility of not doing it. Education was a prime value in our family. My Russian immigrant parents believed that with education you could achieve anything and they sacrificed themselves to give their children every opportunity possible.

The country was deep in the Depression that had begun in 1929. It was 1941, before the December 7th Japanese attack on Pearl Harbor that plunged us into World War II and—paradoxically—was to bring us out of the Depression and into prosperity.

I was next to the last of seven children and money was in shorter supply than ever.

We'd be at Commencement, singing our class song—"Deep Purple" ("When the Deep Purple Falls "Over Sleepy Garden Walls")—I'd be out of high school and then what? I don't remember even talking about it with my parents. There was no way they could help me.

Then, something astonishing happened.

In our town was a businessman from Chicago by the name of Max Gerber. His company—Kokomo Sanitary Pottery—made toilets in Kokomo. Like us, he was a Russian Jew.

Mr. Gerber had been the major contributor toward building a small Reform temple in Kokomo. I was in the first confirmation class of the new temple. Before we had the temple, we celebrated the High Holy Days in services that we held in the Masonic Temple with a student rabbi and cantor from Hebrew Union College in Cincinnati.

I made an appointment with Mr. Gerber. I had no idea what I would say to him. I just knew I needed help.

Ushered into his office at the appointed time, I was intimidated. He was a large stocky man with a swarthy, rectangular face and jowly cheeks. He looked like a gangster. He had a booming voice, gruff to his employees, but he would suddenly break into a hearty guffaw. His voice was soft with me. Maybe he knew how shaky I felt.

What I did was ask his advice—I wanted to go to college and did he have any ideas about how I could accomplish that.

Apparently, he'd made inquiry about me before our meeting and learned that out of a graduating class of some 340, I was to be the valedictorian.

"If you go to a university in the East or the University of Chicago, I'll put you through," he said. Just like that. And that was the marvelous part.

The other side of it was my mother's reaction. When my mother learned what Mr. Gerber had said, she warned, "If you don't work for something, no good comes of it." I wonder now what mix of fears for me and perhaps unconscious mother/daughter jealousies went into that notion. I didn't think to remind her that I had worked to get all A's in high school. Unfortunately, I allowed that injunction to hex the incredible gift I'd been given; too little did I let touch me what I was learning and living. I didn't feel entitled to the good stuff. It took me a lifetime to realize the influence that this witch's message, this lack of entitlement has played in my life—a poison ivy intertwined with . . . stunting . . . the tree of life so that, indeed, the prophecy came to be partly fulfilled. What I'd been given did come to less good than it could have.

I applied only to the University of Chicago and was accepted. I'd never heard of Harvard. There were no guidance counselors in those days. My big brother Misch was living in Chicago then. That was a big draw.

Mr. Gerber was true to his word. I pinched every penny hard before spending it, scrupulously spending as little as possible and after the first year I got a scholarship from the U. of C. Mr. Gerber never questioned my expenses—for tuition, dormitory, meal plans. I never had to tell him twice what I needed. Maybe he was aware that I kept expenses pared to the minimum. I was at the U. of C. for six years, from 1942 to 1948, got a Bachelor's, and a Master's in International Relations with a major in International Law. Unusual as it was in those days for a woman to go on and get a master's, if I'd "known then what I know now" I would have pushed for a doctorate; the devil of it was I was at sea about what I wanted to do.

When I graduated, it didn't' even occur to me to apply to the diplomatic corps since that was only for rich men in those days. I went directly to New York, and right up to TIME Inc. and was hired as a trainee researcher in the International News Department of TIME Magazine. But isn't it something, looking back, that I didn't aim my studies toward a more pragmatic down-to-earth goal? It tells of an underlying assumption of the times that in the end, a woman expected she'd find a man to take care of her.

Those were great years, those years at TIME-LIFE—some of the best times of my life. In another vignette, I tell about what it was like working there in the paternalistic, gender-divided 1940s and '50s when all the writers were men and all the researchers were women.

After I'd been a researcher for a couple of years, I was longing to go to Europe. I mentioned that once to Mr. Gerber. He opened his wallet and peeled off $1500.

I took a leave of absence from TIME and sailed off to Europe on the ocean liner, the Isle de France. I got seasick a lot but I also had many firsts—I was determined to try everything. For instance, I had the first massage of my life—and by a man. I affected grand nonchalance which I'm sure didn't fool the masseur one whit. He was undoubtedly aware of my girlish embarrassment. Many of the young people on board were wearing Bermuda shorts. They were in. I believed—for a reason unknown to me now—that Bermuda shorts and blue jeans were unbecoming on me. So I didn't wear them and felt—once again—the outsider. The haunting music of the movie, *The Third Man,* was playing everywhere all over Western Europe that year. Determined to absorb as much of Europe as possible and stay away from anything American, I didn't see the movie and to this day I've never happened to catch up with it.

I traveled around Western Europe for seven months with two enormous suitcases that included three 1950s style big shouldered, fitted-waist wool suits, white gloves and a girdle as stomachs must always be pulled in to look totally flat. I lugged those blasted heavy albatrosses everywhere. Once, I wanted to get through the Pyrenees mountains from France to Andorra. The people at the French travel office said the snows were too deep. You couldn't get over the Pyrenees between Spain and France at that time of the year.

I did, though. I have a picture of a bullock cart that helped. At that time, there was one person in Andorra who spoke English. She had a little inn, "the Pla." I arrived so cold and shivery I thought I'd never get warm again. Madame Pla had a bath drawn—lots of hot water carried in pails upstairs—and it was magical. Scrumptiously hot. I'll never forget how delicious that hot bath was.

Through the years, I would see Mr. Gerber from time to time when he came to New York. I was always thrilled when he invited me to join him and one or more of his cronies at his hotel or for dinner. I have a memory of his asking me to pour wine for a group of his cronies and later commenting, "You can tell a lot about a person by any one action like the way that person pours wine."

Because he had gout, he couldn't drink alcohol and he had to eat plain food such as boiled chicken, but he took pleasure in seeing people around him enjoying food and drink. He flirted outrageously with waitresses—he was a sensual man—then guffawed uproariously like an overgrown kid at the incredulous look on their faces when they saw the size of the tip.

Sometimes, Mr. Gerber would ask about my love life. Once, I'd met and was ga-ga over a young man from Johannesburg, South Africa, Phillipp Wulfson. He was tall and attractive and he spoke a beautiful English. Showing him around New York, I took him up to the top of the Empire State Building. He kissed me there and my watch stopped. I later mentioned that to Mr. Gerber and he asked, beginning to pull out his wallet, whether I'd like to go to South Africa. I hastily said no. Looking back, I wonder what were the components of that "no." Certainly, fear was in there.

Mr. Gerber was a family man. He and his wife, son Oscar and daughter Harriet lived in Chicago in a plain two-storied stucco house facing Lake Michigan. I was invited there sometimes. Harriet sometimes wanted to give me some of her clothes. Once, she offered me a coat. I said, "I have a coat." That was my memory. But a photograph belies this. I'm wearing a jaunty little wool sport coat that she must have given me. It's the sort of thing I never would have bought myself.

Mr. Gerber once gave me a hammered silver bracelet he'd brought back from Trinidad. Somehow, somewhere, down through the years and many moves, it got lost. It saddens me that I lost it. The catch must have come loose. Telling about the Trinidad bracelet, I'm reminded of another present he gave me—a tiny delicate watch with rubies sprinkled around the face.

I once asked Mr. Gerber how I could ever repay him. "Help others along the way," he replied. Ironically, his only son Oscar was shot dead on a Chicago street, I learned years later. No shape of justice there!

Looking back, I regret that I didn't express enough to Mr. Gerber while he was alive, my tremendous gratitude. I didn't write to him enough from those months in Europe—I felt I had to say something special and wonderful; that an ordinary post card wouldn't do. The need to be Special got in my way. Maybe—I hope—I expressed more gratitude than I remember. Or maybe he knew, anyway.

University of Chicago Days

When I arrived at the University of Chicago I felt like a country hick in a hopeless catch-up task—just as I'd felt I could never catch up, being next to the youngest in our large family. Halfway through my years at the U. of C. I was to have an experience that put a big dent in my Kokomo kid naiveté. More about that later.

My big brother Misch was living in Chicago then. That was a major reason I chose Chicago instead of a school in the East. Misch would often drop by the dorm in the morning for us to go have breakfast together. I'd brush my teeth, douse my face, throw on gray (shapeless) slacks and a big red and black (shapeless) lumber jacket and off we'd go to a corner eatery. In fact, I think I wore that shapeless outfit most of my years there, hiding any feminine charms. (Ah, how the young believe their thighs will always be firm, their eyes will stay big and beautiful, their hair keep its luster. Fastening on minute or nonexistent imperfections, they squander their beauty instead of reveling in it.)

There were all these sophisticated "girls" (that's what we were called then, instead of, as later, after the women's movement, young women). Some of the girls in my dormitory—Beecher Hall—were from big cities like Chicago and New York. The New York ones listened to classical music on radio WQXR (they actually had their own radios and wore cashmere sweaters). One, Eleanor H., stayed out till all hours and by hearsay "went all the way" with her steady boyfriend. She took "speed" to help her stay up all night to cram for exams. She followed a self-designed interdisciplinary course of study. Her major was Philosophy. She seemed the ultra sophisticate in contrast to my hickdom.

My roommate was Hadassah Samuels from Chicago. Her father died of leukemia and maybe partly because of that she decided to become a doctor. She was great on precision and detail. Once she did a dissection of a cat's head, the charming little skeletal skull presided over her desk and our room ever after. When Hadassah came back from visiting her family, she'd be laden with cookies that she shared with all of us. Her mother also sent her packages. She was an only child. (I must confess to feeling jealous because in all my six years there, I never got a box of cookies.)

Hadassah's life work would be spent as a psychiatrist and in her fifties she went back to school for a Master's in Fine Arts to become a painter. This was roughly a mirror-opposite of my own personal and work history; I was in publishing—researcher, reporter, picture editor, editor/writer—and in my fifties went back for another master's as a social worker and became a therapist.

The U. of C. was then under the charismatic sway of the handsome Robert Maynard Hutchins and of such other "Great Books" lights as Mortimer Adler. Many were the gossipy conversations about Hutchins and his artist-wife Maude, with us draped over the dorm bunks. The Hutchins' house was right across the street from Beecher Hall so we sometimes caught glimpses of those luminous beings.

The U. of C. felt huge and impersonal to me. I was lost at first. I don't think they had such a thing as career counselors. If they had women's deans then, I don't remember knowing about them, or about psychotherapy, about "sharing" and venting feelings with peers or counselors. I thought I was all alone in having "bad . . . anxious . . . depressed" feelings.

The U. of C. had a special mystique and a reputation for having top-notch people in their fields. Among them was Norman MacLean who taught English and whose book, published many years later, A River Runs Through It, became a bestseller and movie. On the surface the book was about fly-fishing. Deeper, it was about living life well. Mr. MacLean had a roving eye (literally) and made strange movements with his mouth and face and neck. I don't know what medical condition he had, perhaps Tourettes. But I do know he had a strange gift to draw answers out of me that I didn't know were there. If no one else came up with the answer he was "fishing" for, he'd say, "All right, Isabelle, what is it?" and to my surprise it came out of me as though magnetized.

Richard Peter McKeon was another star when I was at the U. of C. He was a fabulous teacher. A main love of his was Aristotle and a main love of mine was Richard Peter McKeon. He had translated Aristotle. He taught a great course called "Observation, Interpretation and Integration," a tough but splendid philosophy course. Mr. McKeon had a special way of shaping his mouth when he talked and of moving his hands that added to his incredible attractiveness.

There were two noted faculty stars in International Relations, the field I finally settled on, since I didn't have a clue what I wanted to do. Short, squat Quincy Wright, dry and pedantic, and short, wiry and fiery Hans Morgenthau. Morgenthau frequently complained that we didn't read the newspapers assiduously enough. He was my adviser on my Master's thesis. I was fed up with school at that time and did an inferior cut-and-paste job on the subject: "British Diplomacy Regarding the German-Polish Frontier from World War I to 1939," a subject in which I had minimal interest and less knowledge. I have never seen that thesis since then. I did, however, manage to squeak through and received my Master's in International Relations with a major in International Law.

The way the U. of C. curriculum was set up, the Bachelor's (Ph.B. Bachelor of Philosophy) was a two-year degree and consisted of eight courses, four each year in the various fields of knowledge: Humanities, Physical Sciences, Social Sciences, Biological Sciences etc. No grades counted in the course of the year. Everything depended on the four final six-hour exams. The Master's was a three-year program; you could choose to go right through for a Doctorate without getting the Master's, (I was on my way to doing that, but got fed up with going to school, stopped and wrote that abominable thesis). My long suffering adviser on it was the renowned Hans Morgenthau.

It was rare for women to go beyond a Bachelor's, and unfortunately, I wasn't wise enough to see ahead. Besides, I didn't know what I wanted to do. I hadn't discovered my strongest interest.

Living in the dormitory, a certain modicum of civilized behavior was upheld—sort of what I imagine a girls' finishing school might be like. Ferret-faced Miss Tippett was the housemother. At meals, we all waited to lift our forks until she was seated and gave the signal.

Unlike most colleges and universities, there were no curfew rules. The U. of C. considered itself very advanced on that score. Also, there was no football team. The area under the football stadium was used instead in the development of the atom bomb, we learned later.

As in much of my life, I was busy . . . busy . . . busy . . . in many things— theater, for example, and campus activities, including a huge campaign to be the U. of C. delegate to Prague, Czechoslovakia for an international conference. (I came in second in the campus-wide election.) Frenetic activity was then, as in much of my life, a main strategy against connecting with "bad" feelings of depression and anxiety.

Now, as for the experience brought by the summer of 1945. Before heading across country to California with a bunch of friends, I'd promised two men, O. and M. that I would let each know at the end of the summer whether I would marry them. M. was a physicist with Bell Telephone Labs, and was out at Los Alamos that summer, working it turned out, on the atom bomb. I was to stop and see him there at the end of the summer on my way back and tell him my answer. O. was working on his Doctorate in Economics. (I'm reminded here that I'd gone to my brother Misch to get some big brotherly advice on what to do about O.'s kisses. Was it O.K. to kiss with your lips open? Misch's take on it: "if you like it," which seems in retrospect a pretty good answer.)

Each summer I took a job to learn about different fields, e.g. one summer through the help of Mr. Gerber, I worked at *The Chicago Daily News.* In the summer of 1945 Mr. Gerber helped me get a job in Hollywood, working in the Property Department at Universal Studios.

At summer's end I returned to Chicago to learn that my friend F. and my erstwhile swain O. had taken up with each other.

Now, the truth was that my relationship with F. was more important to me than that with O. and my answer to him (as to M.) was to be "No." But F. (out of guilt?) would have nothing to do with me. I lost the relationship with her over this, to my dismay. After F. and O. had married and moved to another country, I tried to correspond with her without success. However, oddly, she did keep up a correspondence with my sister Leanora and when Leanora and her husband went there, they saw each other.

F.'s life with O. was not easy. In the first years of their marriage, her mother-in-law gave F. a hellish time, ordering her about, though F.

had her doctorate and moved very high up in the governmental hierarchy, as did O. In fact, O. was so near the top, it was thought he might have become president if he hadn't been married to a foreigner.

When I went there, I tried to phone F. but got only as far as the servants. F. never got back to me.

On a later trip, I tried again. F. did return my call and she and O. and their daughter and I had lunch together. O. was physically impaired (perhaps a stroke?) F. and their daughter both seemed eager to come to the States to visit me, but it didn't happen. F. and I saw each other a second time, just the two of us, on that trip. She said she hadn't gotten the message from the servants in the earlier visit.

TIME/LIFE Days

My first stint at TIME-LIFE was in the halcyon days at the height of the TIME-LIFE mystique. LIFE was the picture magazine and TIME was the news magazine and a coveted place to work. In the spring of 1948 when I graduated from the University of Chicago, with an M.A. in International Relations and a major in International Law, I moved to New York and into the Greenwich Village YMCA on Eighth Avenue and Twelfth Street. It was Easter weekend. Sunday was a chilly, gray day that set people shivering in their light Easter finery as they paraded on Fifth Avenue.

Next morning I went up to TIME Inc. and applied for a job. I was hired in a six-month researcher/trainee program in the International News Department, my job, to read all the New York newspapers and clip and route stories to the researchers and writers. Paid for reading! In addition to the fun of it, my pay was the grand amount of thirty-five dollars a week. After two months I was promoted to full-fledged researcher. I absolutely loved working for TIME. I kept saying, "And they pay me for this!" At the same time, I secretly felt I was a fraud; they'd find me out. I wasn't up to their caliber. Later in life I would learn that I was not alone in that kind of secret, gnawing belief.

As a researcher, I'd find that when I called up and said I'm with TIME Magazine, people would be galvanized to hop to, to supply the needed information. There was a gratifying sense of power in that, I must admit. Because it was such a coveted job (the pay was somewhat higher—maybe 20 percent higher than elsewhere in publishing) people seemed to give 150 percent of themselves. Not a bad exchange for a company.

In the late 1940s and early 1950s, all the writers were men and all the researchers were women. The researchers sat in open cubicles in what was called, paradoxically, the "bull pen." The writers were in offices with windows and were trained and brought along by the editors—a hierarchy of several layers.

The research staff was presided over by Content Peckham (her real name), a tough cookie, powerful in her fiefdom; a hard-driving lady with the face of an aging patrician beauty. She ruled over the "bull pen" denizens with a steely hand. It seemed surprising to encounter such an august personage in the next stall in the "john."

We researchers supplied the writers with information from our interviews and written sources and then, after the story was written, checked the accuracy of each word of each edited version, applying a dot on each word, a red dot for proper names. Often we had to battle vigorously with the writers and editors when their beloved prose was at odds with the facts as we'd learned and presented them.

We did work hard; each week built to a crescendo toward Monday night's "putting the magazine to bed." We played hard too. Lunches in the early part of the week were sometimes long and leisurely, depending on what needed to be done. Two martini lunches were not uncommon. There were hundreds of restaurants in the vicinity of the TIME-LIFE building. Larre's was one of the nearby French restaurants; for ninety-nine cents you got a four-course lunch that included appetizer, coffee and dessert. One of the dessert choices was a fabulous rum cake worthy of a Viennese pastry shop.

On Monday nights, dinners of our choice were brought up in beguiling little picnic boxes and there was lots of camaraderie among the researchers, writers and editors as we sat at or atop our desks, waiting for each successive edited version. Writers could manage to slip in a wide array of errors while turning the facts into colorful prose. Sparks often flew between writers and researchers as the researchers tried to get the writers to hew to the facts and the writers fought to keep beloved prose.

I remember one late Monday night exchange with a top editor, Max Ways. Max raised his voice when I'd pushed especially hard on a point at issue: "I don't want to see your face in here again tonight." That felt horrible. I went hot all over and fled.

Work life was generally much more relaxed than today. And work wasn't all of life as it too often seems to be nowadays. Sometimes I went horseback riding with a friend in Central Park in the morning before heading to Rockefeller Center. Now people work longer and harder, tethered to tyrannical beepers and cellular phones. Then there were all kinds of playtime events for the employees. We had bowling teams. We put on plays. One such was Thornton Wilder's *Our Town.* I had the role of town gossip Mrs. Soames, a part I'd also played in high school and in college. There were lavish TIME-OUT parties galore where the employees were sumptuously fed and feted. Some got slightly drunk and more than slightly flirtatious. Hanky-panky sometimes accompanied these parties.

At one such full day at a country club, one sleek young woman wearing a white dress with black polka dots, was very sought after. I wanted such a dress and looked for one later but never found it. I do have a snapshot of me at that party in a bathing suit standing on the shoulders of Henry Anatole Grunwald who went on to become the top editor of TIME Magazine and later the ambassador to Austria.

I remember in particular, one writer, Jack, a portly, florid, middle-aged married man who used to come early and stay late at all the shindigs. He used to rock on his heels, surveying the current crop of young women, and make cheery advances and laugh high and dryly when they turned him down. One year, his line to me was "You're the most feminine woman I've ever seen." Subsequently, he failed to notice my femininity or me at all as he rocked and beamed his ingratiating smile toward the current candidate. Each year, as his paunch thickened, he picked younger, svelte women.

A favorite topic of TIME Inc'ers—reminiscent of college dormitory "bull sessions"—was gossip and tale-telling about the founders of TIME and LIFE, Henry Luce, his confreres, and his celebrated wife, Claire Boothe Luce. Claire Boothe had authored a play, The Women, a scathing look at women that pre-dated the women's' movement. There was both a desire to ride on the Luces' celebrity and simultaneously an urge to cut them down.

There was talk—sometimes with a sneer—about TIME Inc's "paternalism." Today we could use a little of that scorned paternalism in corporate life where security and loyalty have vanished, where many employees are forced into contract work.

The newspaper guild was a powerful force representing the workers. I remember long, tedious shop meetings as our unit of the Newspaper Guild negotiated hard with management. The Guild was a powerful force to be reckoned with in those days. We sometimes had to resort to picketing.

TIME Magazine editorial people were off Tuesday and Wednesday in those days, after the magazine "went to bed" on Monday nights—often very late. We were compensated for the uncommon schedule with four weeks vacation a year plus a week off every thirteenth week. I got used to the luxury of so much time off, sometimes expunging dreary February from the calendar and spending the month in the Caribbean.

Social life did tend to become somewhat incestuous because of TIME Magazine's schedule. Several of us wound up renting a summerhouse together on Fire Island. I had an experience that still tightens my belly when I think of it. A bunch of us were on the beach. I went out swimming with a man I particularly liked—Bob S.—but didn't ever try for, assuming I had no chance with him. (That old familiar self defeating core belief.) Suddenly, I realized I was caught in an undertow and was being carried far out. Bob was getting smaller and smaller. People on the beach, far in the distance, were continuing to sun themselves and play volleyball. Against the thunderous pounding of the surf they couldn't hear my cries for help. Finally, a lifeguard did spot us and he ran out and started pulling me in on a rope. It was dreadful being pulled through the water. I couldn't breathe. He got me to the beach and laid me down and—I don't remember—I guess pumped out the water. But I do remember that I went blind for awhile. I guess some sort of hysterical reaction. It took a few minutes before my sight returned. My friend Pat Ogden saw all the commotion with people running down to the water's edge and said, "Oh look they're saving someone," and then, coming closer, saw that I was the one being rescued.

I've always had a strong respect for the power of the ocean since, and have always worried about it for my two children. Josh now scuba dives and though I don't want to taint his fun with my worry, I'm always glad when he has returned safely. I've known my daughter Melanie to swim all the way across a sizable lake without a buddy.

I will say that I've never worked in another publishing house where the caliber of the employees was so universally high. Many people came and went repeatedly, never finding as satisfactory and exciting a workplace. TIME Inc. had a reputation for hiring back its people. I worked there in three different stints adding up to eleven years—1948 to 1954, 1965 to 1967 and 1974 to 1977.

Once, after being away I ran into one of the TIME Inc. librarians in the elevator. "Haven't seen you around for awhile. Have you been on vacation?" he said breezily. I'd been away seven years.

In TIME Inc. elevators, one often caught lively snatches of conversation. One morning a woman got in wearing a raincoat. Some one said, "Hey, the sun's shining. Why are you wearing a raincoat?" "It was raining when I left London," she shot back.

After working a couple of years in the International News Department of the magazine, I took a leave of absence in 1950—it ended up stretching to seven months—and traveled around Western Europe—including Spain, Austria, France, Italy, Switzerland and all the little principalities—Andorra, Liechtenstein, San Marino, Luxembourg, and Monaco. I was curious how these principalities had managed to survive as independent countries over time, and I wrote pieces about them that were published in my hometown newspaper, *The Kokomo Tribune.* I didn't think of offering them to TIME Inc.

That summer my brother Misch and his wife Lore came over to Paris and we shared an apartment, a seventh floor walk-up with a toilet at the end of the hall whose light never stayed on long enough. But it was on the left bank and had a view of the Eiffel Tower. Misch, an artist, primarily a printmaker, has exhibited throughout the world and is spoken of in art books as a pioneer printmaker. He succeeded in making my parents proud. He used the same Paris print atelier that Picasso, Alexander Calder and his close friend, British printmaker Stanley (Bill) Hayter were using.

When I returned to New York I asked to switch from International News to "floating in the Back of the Book"—art, music, theatre, science, etc. This meant getting to go to theatre, art and music openings. Later I moved on to become a reporter with the MARCH OF TIME. MOT was a newsreel shown in movie theatres while the main feature film was re-wound. The stentorian voice of Westbrook Van Voorhees announced The March of Time.

Working for MOT was a real kick. We had lots of freedom and flexibility. If you got an idea and a yen to do a particular show, you'd make a case for producing it and you might get a go-ahead. For example, I proposed doing a show on contemporary American art and artists. So I researched the idea. I went up to visit "Sandy" Calder at his Connecticut home and studio. His enormous studio was a phantasmagorical universe, jam-packed with his colorful and wonderful, witty and whimsical moving sculptures. I interviewed him—a wonderful man, a mixture of pixie and huggable bear, full of life and energy and often liquor—and developed the shape of the segment he'd be in and then worked with the camera crew on the shooting. Another American artist we did a segment on in that film was James Brooks, a foremost abstract expressionist of the time. His wife Charlotte Brooks was, in my view, a better artist than her husband, but in those times, it was he—the male—who was taken seriously.

When MOT suspended operations in 1954, I left TIME Inc. and got a series of jobs in other publishing houses—including Doubleday, Grolier (where I was Director of Photography for a three-year re-make of the twenty-volume *Book of Knowledge),* American Heritage and Horizon magazines. But I would return again and again to TIME, drawn by the pleasure of working with so many smart, savvy people.

In the middle 1960s, I was hired as a picture editor, designing picture essays in Time Inc.'s *The Great Ages of Man* series—beautiful books and a treat to work on. I dispatched photographers all over the world. Too bad I hadn't yet taken up photography myself. I was working three days a week and my staff people were working full-time. It was just too time-consuming to keep catching up each week with what had gone on in my days away. I was asked to work full-time. I had married in 1957. Our two children, Josh and Melanie, were then eight and four. Too young for me to work full-time. Again, I left. A wrench between fulfilling work and motherly duties.

In 1974 I returned and applied for a job as a picture editor. There was no opening for a picture editor. They offered me a job as a writer/editor in the book division. "I'm not a writer," I said. "Don't worry about it," they said. The irony is, in the 1940s and 1950s when all the writers were men and all the researchers were women, the women mostly didn't even aspire to be writers. They knew they just didn't have IT—the requisite male "equipment." And they weren't brought along, learning the craft of writing. This hiring thus reflected a major tectonic shift taking place, largely as a result of the women's movement.

The Women's Movement

I was living in Westchester County, north of Manhattan in a beautiful big home with four bathrooms(!)with my lawyer husband, partner in a New York law firm, our two young children and a storybook surface.

In the latter 1960s following publication of Betty Friedan's Feminine Mystique, the Women's' Movement took hold. Consciousness-Raising groups sprung up. I remember vividly the first "CR" group I went to. There were thirty-some of us attending. The topic of the evening was "personal appearance:" our feelings and thoughts about it. We went around the circle and each woman had a chance to speak to the topic. That was the format that developed for "CR" groups.

A remarkable eye opener that night was the commonality of concern and the amount of energy put into appearance, and the lack of acceptance and satisfaction most women felt about their bodies and looks, even beautiful women. Thighs were too big, not big enough. One was too skinny or too fat. Never just right. Those who were considered beautiful now, by the standards of our society, feared loss of that beauty as they aged.

The group split up into small groups of around eight. We met monthly in each others' homes—exploring a different topic each month— and continued to meet, typically, for about a year and a half, the usual life span of "CR" groups. Instead of looking down on women, women began to appreciate other women: "sisterhood is powerful" became a catch phrase.

I remember some of my own sisters and friends scoffing at women who joined such groups.

"I am liberated" and "I'm not a groupie" maintained some.

"Men will stop opening doors for women and performing other acts of chivalry," said some.

"It's worth the loss of that sort of chivalry for women to gain real power," was the response.

Money issues were popular group discussion topics. I remember some women in our affluent Westchester community, admitting openly that, though their marriages were not what they'd like, they had many benefits—beautiful homes, much travel and the rest of the good life. They weren't about to let go of that.

Some did let go, got divorced (myself included). Some discovered that satisfaction lay in lesbian relationships. There was a lot of unraveling.

Many men were vulnerable, confused, off-balance. They couldn't see then that there could be gains for them, too, as women became empowered.

My hero and a model to many of us in our struggles was Gloria Steinem. Born to a middle-class, single-parent family, Steinem went to the barricades against stereotypical men-women relationships. Though abandoned physically by her father and psychologically by her manic-depressive mother, she was an original and audacious thinker and writer. To gain information for her mission of slaying dragons of our society, she descended into the underworld—the

Playboy Club—disguised as a bunny and emerged to expose the exploitation of women.

Steinem recognized the importance of language in perpetuating our ways of thinking, originated the non-gender title of Ms., and started Ms. Magazine to aid the process of educating women. Her writings, lectures, and public demonstrations, in raising the consciousness of women, brought a deeper awareness of the domination of our society by males.

If hero Steinem didn't actually slay the reactionary dragons of entrenched power (the likes of Orrin Hatch, Robert Dole, Strom Thurmond, Jesse Helms), she did direct a powerful searchlight on them.

As with most heroes down through time, Steinem's journey took her into the lower depths. At one point she succumbed to burn-out and withdrew from society and work. Her male companion stood by her during her dark period of illness and self-doubt. She came back with renewed strength and wrote a book on self-esteem.

By her example and writings, Steinem challenged male supremacy and catalyzed women to reach toward empowerment.

Our society has undergone such rapid change in the past few decades. We forget what it was like so recently. (For example, as recently as 1974 when I went to buy a house after the break-up of my marriage, my signature wouldn't work. I had to have the signature of my divorcing husband on the deed.)

Changes have come remarkably, unbelievably swiftly since the upheavals of those early consciousness-raising days.

Women—and men—often seem to take for granted the gains made as a result of those tempestuous times.

MAKING MY WAY IN THE WORLD

As adults we all deal with the question of how we will get what we need to survive and be happy. These stories show some of my experiences as I learned to "make my way" in the world.

The Lesson

Icy winter day. Crossing the Bronx Whitestone Bridge, returning to Manhattan. Suddenly, my brakes fail.

Fortunately, I'm coming slowly up to the toll booth when it happens. And the road grade helps me stop. Also, fortunately, there chances to be a policeman there. He helps me get the car over on the shoulder. I phone AAA. They say they'll send someone out. An hour later. Frozen. Still no AAA. I phone a second time. They have no record of the first call. They'll send someone out. An eternity. I phone AAA again. Yes, they'll send someone, though they have no record of either of the first two calls. The cop had warned me that under these conditions, that could happen and that I should just keep calling. Finally, the AAA does actually arrive in the form of a junk heap of a tow truck, driven by a Chinese man who looks like a Fu Manchu right out of Central Casting.

As I climb in the cab beside him, he announces emphatically in a surprisingly high thin voice that I'll have to pay cash. I'm not about to tell him I haven't any. I want to get-the-heck back with my car to Westchester and my Mamaroneck service station, not leave the car stranded, to be dismembered by human vultures.

When we get to Larchmont, I "discover" I don't have the cash. I tell him to stop at Citibank. Alas, the unfriendly ATM won't oblige. It says—heartlessly—there's no money in the account. A deposit hasn't cleared.

I plead with him to take a check. He won't budge.

We drive further. He's getting more and more agitated.

We reach my house. Blessed moment. I go in to phone neighbors, friends. No cash. I pretend that maybe my garage will be open (in order to get him to tow the car there, so I won't have another tow fee in the morning). He falls for it and we go there. They're closed, of course. But I heave a sigh of relief. I've managed to get the car back home to my service station.

But now he goes hysterical. He punches his head against the steering wheel and the side of the car and bites his own arm and screams pitifully. He says his boss will fire him. I say, trying to remain reasonable, "I'll talk with your boss for you." He screams and rages. He says, "I don't have his telephone number . . . the Boss is a Jew. Nothing but money means anything to him. I work for $150 a week because I can't find another job," he says. I let that go in the interest of achieving my goal of getting myself and my car home. Then he threatens to tow the car back to the Bronx.

At this, I suddenly realize he has been demonstrating how to behave. So I get fake hysterical and start screaming and crying. And just as suddenly he calms down, unhooks the car from the truck and we go back into my house. He stomps in, I have a moment of fear, call the AAA, and they agree to stand behind my check, which will be O.K. the next day. I write out the check for the exact amount—$59.63. (He had been threatening to charge me monstrous amounts of bucks waiting-time for the gyrations described which lasted some twenty to twenty-five minutes.)

Transformed, calm, he gives a courtly bow from the waist, gestures with his hand as though removing it from a flowing Manchu sleeve, waddles contentedly out my living room door and down the front steps into the bitter cold night.

The Prism

Journal, May, 1970. Must get this started while I can. Those blue pills dope me up. Being in the hospital is like being in a universe that's a combination of Pinter, Ionesco, Chaplin, Kafka and Bergman.

My right arm has slipped out of the traction again. They don't know how to fix it right. But at least I now have these wonderful mirrored prism glasses. Been in bed without being able to read for three weeks now with a bad back that resulted from a strenuous March on Washington to demonstrate against the Vietnam War.

And just today I learned about these special prism glasses that enable one to read while lying down. (Wouldn't you think that the orthopedic surgeon or someone would tell a traction patient about such helpful things?) Of course, I was desperate to get a pair. I learned that a certain optometrist in the nearby village of Portchester sold them, but the question was how to get a pair delivered. It's late Saturday afternoon. Everybody's out.

In pain and in traction, everything is so unwieldy and difficult. And I'm doped up with those blue pills. I manage to phone the optometry shop. A breathy sexy female voice answers. When I ask for the proprietor, she says tartly he's out to lunch. Somehow from the way she says it, I get the vibes that's not exactly true. I put on an authoritative voice, "Dr. Grant (orthopedic doctor) asked me to speak with Dr. Copeland." A lie.

Taught never to lie. But have to lie to survive. At that, Doctor C. comes to the phone making munching noises. Chicken, he informs me. As it's late Saturday afternoon, if I don't get those glasses this afternoon, I'll have to wait to be able to read until Monday morning. Interminable.

My leaping fantasy; the female voice is of his pretty young dumb-ass-blond (hey, now there's a Freudian slip) secretary/assistant whom he has largely for decorative effect.

And is he, classically, miserably married to that wife who makes the lunch he's munching?

It's 1970. I'm deep into consciousness raising. It goes against my principles to put on the femaleness with a heavy hand, sexy sounding, submissive so he can be the generous, big, powerful male. But I must get those glasses this afternoon.

I tell him my problem. I'm desperate to get a pair of those prism glasses this afternoon, having just learned about them. Please, could he bring a pair to the hospital for me.

A stony "No" greets this idea. "Can't do it. No time." Yet, something comes through between the words. Is he a bit of a lady-killer (old fashioned idea but perhaps true)? Susceptible to flirting? "What shape are you in?" (Ha! My intuition was right on.) "My husband thinks I'm in good shape." (What a vamp; but I must have those glasses.)

"What are you in the hospital for?" (Interesting implications to that question. One step forward.)

"Traction for a cervical disk."

"How long?"

"A week to ten days."

"We're open till five o'clock. Have your husband pick up the glasses."

(One giant step back.)

"He can't. He's stuck at the office in a crisis." A not unusual circumstance for a lawyer.

A pause.

Fantasies, his and mine. I know what mine are. Finally, he agrees to bring the prism glasses to me in the hospital.

I try to slick myself up. I couldn't reach the deodorant so I sprayed the perfume under my hairy arms and slathered lipstick on my chapped lips, powdered my nose, brushed my hair. I did the best I could. Unfortunately, the damn traction device squeezes my face up something fierce. I look grotesque. My worst feature, my nose, is the most prominently displayed part of my anatomy. My best features, my blue eyes, are all pinched up weirdly, my hair, all shapeless from lying down.

End of story. He brings in the prism glasses. I pay him. I get to read. Bliss.

I try to make up to my conscience for my consciousness-raising lapses. It was in a good cause, I rationalize, and nobody was harmed. Fantasies are fine. It's what you do with them that counts.

Two Whiskers

(To preserve anonymity, this case is a composite.)

My first job after graduating from social work school was in a hospital in Westchester, New York. I didn't want to do medical social work because it meant primarily discharge planning rather than psychotherapy but I took what I could get in the tight job market of that time, 1982. After thirty years in publishing, much of it with TIME-LIFE, I'd gone back to school for another Master's to train as a social worker with the goal of becoming a psychotherapist. My job was not without some satisfactions, for each case was a fascinating life story. It's long been a passion of mine, even before I became a psychotherapist, to learn peoples' life stories. A one-time "boy friend" of mine used to tease me, saying that we'd enter a restaurant and within five minutes of ordering our meal I'd be deeply involved in the life story of a person at the next table. Frustration on the job came from not being able to get deeply into each person's story because of time pressure. Still, despite the nerve-wracking juggling of countless details, some cases irresistibly drew me in.

One such was Miss U. The first time I saw Miss U. she was reading Zola's *Nana* in French from a hand-tooled leather book. She seemed to have no hesitation about asking me to tweeze two coarse whiskers from her chin (one white and one gray). Miss U. seemed the sort who felt entitled to get what she wanted. An eighty-nine year old patrician lady, she had been living and sleeping on one chair in one corner of the huge library room of a crumbling twenty-two room mansion, a house so immense that human squatters lived in parts of it. The records of visiting nurses noted that the floors were rotted and disintegrating. She had come into the hospital malnourished and skeletal. Miss U. had cancer of the rectum and had had a colostomy. In a case conference, our team decided she should go to a skilled nursing facility. Told of this team decision, she refused. Positively. She insisted on being discharged home.

In constant attendance on Miss U. was B., a eunuch-looking young man perhaps in his thirties. (I don't really have any idea what a eunuch looks like, but that's the word that occurred to me whenever I saw or spoke with this young man.) Overweight. Pasty-face. Toad-like neck. Short, pear-shaped body. Tight, tremulous voice. Self-involved, self-pitying, weepy. But Miss U. glowed like a school girl when B. was near her.

Despite the difficulties of arranging things so that Miss U. could attain her desire, my task was to work toward home discharge. That's what the lady wanted; the principle of Self Determination is to social workers what Scout's Honor is to scouts. It was my bounden duty to try to carry out her wishes. There was no working telephone or stove. No heat. No electricity. Gargantuan efforts were involved. I made numerous phone calls to her nearest relative, a nephew in Colorado, and was back and forth (twenty-five times in one day alone) with a local agency that sent nurses and cleaning help and arranged to get a new stove and linoleum etc. Done.

After a couple of days at home, however, Miss U. took a turn for the worse. The nurse called the doctor. The doctor said, "Call an ambulance to take her back to the hospital."

Miss U. was having none of that. She was determined to die at home with her beloved Mr. B. "Kiss me, B," she said, he told me later. And as he did, she left the shell of her troublesome body behind. Gone. Miss U. had once again gotten what she wanted.

The obituary in the local paper reported that Miss U. had been a Suffragette, a lawyer in the 1920s, a director of banks and hospitals. She had crossed the Atlantic dozens of times. She had been scheduled to sail on the Titanic when plans had been changed. She died in the house in which she had been born. "Surviving," said the obituary, was "her friend of many years, Mr. B."

Later, when I phoned Mr. B. to ask if there was anything I could do to help him (he'd been seen wandering about on the street) he said dazedly, "What will become of me? There's no one to look after me."

Walter Mitty, Move Over

Recently, I had a rush of revelation why some people call in false fire alarms.

After moving into my new condo, in a turn-of-the century six-unit triple decker in Cambridge, I'd been having throat pain, hoarseness, and some respiratory problems and had been trying to get at the cause. I first went the traditional route, since I'm paying my good money as an HMO subscriber. I saw an allergist.

"You don't have an allergy. You can't develop an allergy after you're forty," he pronounced. ("NEXT")

Next, an ear, nose, throat M.D. She looked down my throat with a nasty wiggly tube with a light at the tip. "You don't have a polyp" she said. ("NEXT")

Next I called some city agencies. "Does any department check air quality to determine the presence and level of pollutants (and if the air is suitable for breathing)?" I might have added. Seems the Boston environment office does but Cambridge doesn't.

After a number of blind alleys and the usual frustrating phone waits and robot-idiot messages and getting stuck in computer loops and having to listen to jangly music and endless commercials, I happened on an actual human being who suggested I call the fire department, that they can check air quality.

I looked for a non-emergency number in the phone book. Couldn't find one. Only 911. Phoned the operator. Got a number. Do I have the non-emergency fire department number?" I asked hastily.

"Yes."

"I understand you check air quality." And I explained that I'm having some difficulty with my throat and some respiratory distress. Before I could finish, the man at the other end of the phone asked my address and barked: "Someone will be there in a few minutes." (CLICK) Shortly, a knock on the door. Firemen are swarming there in the hallway. "Omigod. It's not an emergency." I say.

"That's what people say sometimes when it is."

They throw questions at me. My hands and face feel clammy. One young fireman, obviously trained in body language, points out that I look pale and sweaty. An older seasoned man says it could be just from all the people and excitement.

"Why are you touching your chest?" asks one youth. "Will you get into the ambulance?" says a sandy-haired young man who looks about twelve years old. "We'll take you to any hospital you want to go, including Cambridge Hospital." (I learned a few minutes later that that ride of a few yards would have cost me $225.)

They do—yes—measure the carbon monoxide level and determine that that's O.K. (but check for nothing else in the air quality).

Some of the platoon are finally dismissed to go back to the station.

Others continue to stomp about in their seven-league cuffed boots looking in the nooks and crannies of the apartment.

At first it makes me almost physically ill to see what I've wrought.

Some of the men insist I go out on the front porch and sit in the fresh air. I do and then I see the ambulance and line of fire trucks stretching down the street and the line of cars having to wait. Young sandy-hair continues to recommend the ambulance.

I sit on the front stoop watching the action.

And suddenly an epiphany. What a shot of adrenaline it could be . . . what a sense of power . . . to precipitate the eruption of all this action . . . all these men scurrying about, holding up impatient drivers, causing neighbors' speculation: "Is someone dead . . . dying . . . about to be rushed to the emergency room?" Yes, indeed. What power.

And what an antidote to the daily frustrations and sense of powerlessness, to the endless waiting . . . in traffic . . . on the phone: "Your call is important to us. Please stay on the line . . . your call is important to us . . . Please stay on the line." And all the other numbing frustrations in the course of an ordinary day. Umm, yes, what power and how enticing.

Walter Mitty, move over. Next time I get that old familiar frustrated, powerless feeling, I have a ready fantasy.

MEN AND WOMEN

Love and sex—most of us want them. And for most of us they're a challenge. Here are some of the ironies and idiosyncrasies I've encountered as I've navigated the waters of romance.

Stanley's Peek

Stanley was short and squat and had a round face and sweated a lot. Once when we'd been out to dinner together—these were my early years in New York— and he'd come upstairs with me afterwards, he lingered and lingered.

I finally said, "I have to go to bed. Tomorrow's a workday."

"Please let me tuck you in. I just want to see you without your clothes on. Then I'll leave."

I decided I could stand to have some admiration, even if it was just from Stanley. Stanley had been "sweet on me" for a long time.

I undressed and quickly slid under the covers.

His voice got all gravelly and he said, "You're so beautiful." I knew it in a way. I had a tiny waist that I called attention to by the dresses I wore. But I was self-conscious about my small boobs.

Dutifully, he left as he'd promised.

I went right to sleep.

La Ronde

My last night in Athens. I'm having ouzo in a taverna with Roger, a Frenchman I'd met that afternoon in the Painting Museum when I turned to him—I had to spill out my delight to someone—to exclaim about the fascinating Magritte sculpture of an enormously fat man, seated, with a huge bird cage in the middle of his body.

Now, looking around the taverna, I notice at the table next to ours a pinch-faced, well-dressed middle-aged man with a mustache, a paunch and an expectant air.

In saunters a young man in a creamy-white suit, spots him and heads for his table. The older man's eyes light up, his face becomes animated. He pats strands of hair on his forehead and pulls in his paunch. They talk. The older man, beaming and ingratiating, leans toward the young man. The young man lounges back lazily, accepting his fawning attention.

Soon, in comes another young man with tight jeans, shirt open to reveal his chest. He looks around, sees the two and heads for their table. The two young men greet each other with easy familiarity and talk together animatedly. The older man, eclipsed, alternately leans back crossing his arms, then forward to try to inject himself into the conversation.

Now, a middle-aged woman enters. She sees the three and walks toward them. She is tightly corseted, tightly coiffed, unsure of her welcome. She sits down at their table amid surface politeness.

Whenever the woman offers anything into the conversation, the middle-aged man makes a dismissive gesture.

With a sudden movement and a word of explanation tossed over his shoulder, the first young man gets up, waves airily to the three of them and goes off to visit acquaintances at another table. The light in the middle-aged man's eyes fades. The second young man, straightening his collar and surreptitiously adjusting his crotch, follows the movements of the first young man out of the corner of his eye while listlessly engaging in conversation with the woman.

After considerable flitting from table to table, the first young man, fully aware of his power, swaggers back to the table. The three figures respond to their puppeteer; they dangle and dance at the end of his strings.

My companion—Roger—and I share with lifted eyebrows our experience of the drama being enacted in the small universe next to us. Roger has told me, in our brief acquaintance—refreshingly—that he has a "happy" marriage. Yet, as he gestures, his arm brushes lightly against my breast, as though accidentally. I wonder briefly what I'll choose to do later.

I glimpse a woman at a nearly table gazing our way. What does she see of these little dramas?

Happy Hour

Provincetown, Cape Cod . . .

Sunset, Sunday evening . . .

A man and a woman sit at an ocean-side bar . . .

"I'll have a piña colada," the woman says to the waiter. She's feeling satisfied and languorous and relishing the anticipation of the drink's sweet coolness.

"The same."

The departing waiter's hip movements are choreographic, the woman notices with amusement.

The man begins to toss fistfuls of salted peanuts into his mouth, one right after the other. What's up, she wonders. It's not like him. He generally watches his calories.

"What's up?" she asks.

He clears his throat. "I need to tell you something." He seems to have gone into deep misery. "I want to be your friend."

"So why the gloom?"

" . . . not your lover."

"Now you tell me," she begins, with a weak attempt to lighten the scene that is fast turning dismal.

His chiseled aquiline nose is gorgeously outlined by the sun. His lean body is so beautiful. She longs to hold him, quiet him, soothe him, silence this talk. She'd thought this was the first of many weekends stretching ahead. How could two people be having such totally different experiences at the same time? Rashomon, always Rashomon.*

"I've found that whenever romance comes into it," he says, "it ruins the friendship. All the romances of my life have been disasters. I want you to stay in my life . . . I'm sorry I lost my head . . . got carried away there for a bit. I should have told you this earlier . . . I want to be your friend."

The waiter reappears. He pays elaborate attention to placement of the piña coladas and replenishing the peanuts that are fast disappearing. He carefully readjusts the piña colada in front of the man, gives him a long look.

"Enjoy," he says softly.

Silently, the woman screams.

*Rashomon is a classic Japanese film that depicts a single event . . . a rape . . . and the four differing views of that event by the four individuals involved.

Out in the Cold

Something surprising happened after I'd quite given up the possibility. I met someone. After fourteen years since the end of my first marriage, I was up at a little inn in New England for a weekend with my friend Midge. He, Bob, was there with his son and daughter-in-law. Nice looking but with a bit of a worried look. Furrowed brow. Neat beard. Good old well-worn L. L. Bean clothes. The three of them were at the bar. My friend Midge and I were playing a relaxed, non-competitive game of Monopoly at a nearby table. When a hotel piece fell and skittered along the floor in his direction, he gallantly retrieved it for us. I wondered later: the fates taking a hand?

"He's interested in you," Midge said. "Why don't you join them at the bar?" I did, after awhile. The daughter-in-law, very self-involved, was talking non-stop about her career and job search. The son seemed easy-going. The two young people were sitting between the two of us. Bob didn't move to a position to make it easier for us to talk. I wondered whether he was the passive sort.

Finally, I said I was going to turn in. At that, Bob, seemingly galvanized, challenged me to a game of Monopoly at seven in the morning, before going off cross-country skiing. A rather weird proposition, I thought. But definitely not passive. I just laughed.

That evening at dinner, Bob materialized at our table. "You didn't show up this morning for our Monopoly game," he chided. He then seemed caught up in my conversation with Midge about my friend Nada and her being in love with a man who always keeps two women on his string at once. I had strong opinions on the matter, which I did not fail to express: Nada should get herself out of that situation instead of putting up with crumbs.

On Sunday morning, before our departures, the talkative daughter-in-law asked for my card; then Bob did too. I wondered: would he have if she hadn't?

That was the end of that story, I thought. He's cute and has a good body, but is GU (geographically undesirable). He lives seven hours away.

Surprise! The following Wednesday he phoned. He had a consulting job— he's an engineer and a Cornell University professor emeritus—just two hours away from where I lived in Westchester County, and could he come visit Saturday. It was not at all convenient that day but I somehow sensed that he would be easily put off by a rejection and probably never call again. So I said "Yes, come for lunch."

He came laden with wine, flowers and brown eggs. He explained to me that he kept chickens as pets and can identify which chicken laid which egg from its color and shape.

After lunch, he announced, "I'm looking for a wife." How refreshing such a forthright, ingenuous declaration was, in contrast to the fear of commitment of many, if not most New York men. He had been widowed after thirty years of marriage, just after he took early retirement so that he and his wife could travel. His wife was in an automobile accident, went into a coma, and died. By his report, he and his wife had never had a difference of opinion. I asked him how it had been for him these past years since his wife Mary's death—socializing with women.

"I had one important relationship that lasted two and a half years, soon after Mary's death. But it's over," he said. When he spoke of this woman—it was with a combination of gratitude because she had opened him to psychological insights, and an undertow of bitterness that I couldn't make sense of. It was he who had ended the relationship presumably because of her over-involvement with an adult son who lived with her.

An interchange about control that took place over tea later, might have given me pause. I managed to ignore it. But I was swept away by the honesty of his answer when I asked him, "What was Mary like?"

"I would have said quiet," he said, "until awhile after she was gone. I realized then that though she was quiet with me, she was lively with her women friends." (uh, oh) What I took from this, ignoring other implications, was that he's a perceptive man who's growing.

"I don't expect to duplicate what I've had," he said. I'm ready for something and someone very different."

After our first lunch rendezvous, there were daily phone calls—sometimes several a day, and beautifully written letters. Quickly a pattern developed of visits "every ten days" (his engineering exactitude) "to keep up the momentum." I was pursued and royally wooed.

One weekend, when we met to go skiing and snowshoeing in the Adirondacks, I said "I'd never get seriously involved with anyone unless he thought I was the cat's pajamas." That evening, as we were snowshoeing back to the lodge, he said with endearing fervor, "I think you're the cat's pajamas."

He was eager for me to see his house in upper New York State. It turned out to be a big white drafty rambling country house with a big country kitchen in a little village. I marveled at the variety and scope of his interests and projects—stamp collecting, carpentry, astronomy, piano and cello-playing, wine-making. He showed me rooms full of his projects of a lifetime, from the first cigar box crystal radio he'd made as a young boy. It worked but remained forever unfinished.

He'd thought of everything romantic for my visit. Flowers, candlelight. Even pink "Caress" soap.

"I'm the man for you," he declared, his certainty dissolving my reserve.

Three weeks after meeting, we began house hunting.

Three months afterwards, we became engaged.

Three months later, we were married.

The wedding was officiated jointly by a little male Rabbi and a large Unitarian woman Minister, since Bob was a Unitarian. I wore a one hundred year-old purple, red and white Japanese kimono that Melanie and I found in a little shop on Cape Cod, in Provincetown. It was a great celebration. All my five sisters and their spouses attended. (My brother didn't as was his usual practice for our family events.) My two children—Melanie and Josh—were there and Bob's sister, mother, four children, three grandchildren (and two more on the way). Family and friends took part reading poems and parts of the ceremony that Bob and I had planned.

And so . . . Bob sold his big house, I sold my townhouse, and we bought a lovely old farmhouse in northern Westchester County, on the crest of a hill with a re-done open plan on the inside, flooded with light, a pond with raucous bullfrogs and a resident family of ducks, an apple tree in the front yard, and the backyard opening onto a huge nature preserve and woods enough to get lost in. We could ski from our back door.

We seemed to have the makings of bliss.

But soon after our marriage, a strange metamorphosis occurred. Resentment, anger, and irritation came from Bob. The same expression that had appeared on Bob's face at mention of his former lover, became a frequent look. What was happening?

One day, into my head popped a review of a Broadway play. I couldn't remember the author or the name of the play, and I hadn't seen it, but the gist of it, from what I remembered of the review, was that after the death of his first wife, a man "falls in love," wants to marry at once. They do, then immediately on the honeymoon, he turns angry, hostile, resentful and rejecting toward his new wife. No one I asked remembered the play.

Then, one night Bob and I went with friends to a nearby community theatre. The footlights came up, the dialogue began and I poked Bob and our friends excitedly: "This is it! This is the play I've been trying to remember the name and author of." It was Neil Simon's Chapter Two. But being a Neil Simon play, the problem having been stated, it gets easily, quickly and smoothly resolved. The protagonist comes to the realization that he resents his new wife's happiness and doesn't want to forget his first wife, as though to allow himself to be happy would be disloyal to wife number one, and would mean he must forget her. He simply has this epiphany, makes an about-face, and they live happily ever after.

In reality, this story had really happened to author Simon; the problem didn't dissolve as easily as in the play. He and his second wife divorced.

I took out a copy of the play from the library, but Bob had no interest in reading or talking about it.

In the course of celebrating our second anniversary, came a chilling premonition. We'd gone up to a little inn in Vermont. To loosen the kinks from the long drive and work up an appetite for dinner, we went for a walk. The air was pungent with autumn smells, the ground crunchy with autumn leaves. We found ourselves walking through a graveyard. As the evening deepened to indigo, a melancholy seemed to wrap itself around my husband. We returned to the inn and its crackling fire and sherry and the cheery fireplace talk with other guests.

The next morning, he seemed not to have shaken off his dark mood of the night before. When I questioned him, he reluctantly told a fragment of a dream he'd had that night; his first wife, Mary, was out in his van—out in the cold. He felt he should go out and be with her. He told the dream without feeling.

One day at tea-time, Bob said mournfully, "We've been married three years and I haven't made a major accomplishment as I'd hoped to when I retired."

"What is it you want to accomplish?" I said, offering him a slice of his own delicious pumpkin pie.

"I don't know."

He was soon to go off for a month alone driving cross-country and hiking in the Rocky Mountains.

"Maybe while you're away you'll have a chance to think about it," I said mildly.

When he returned, the subject didn't come up.

Many small projects pleasantly filled his days chockablock. If only he—and we—could just give up the idea that we must accomplish something outstanding, world-shaking, grand—and could just simply enjoy the small daili-ness of life without poisoning it by the urge to produce something that captures the world's attention! How often the thirst to stand out, to be Special, robs us of the joys of living in the moment, and of our true uniqueness.

Our parting came after being together five years. It was amicable—as amicable as such a painful thing can be. "I realize I want to go back to upper New York State where I spent my life," Bob said. "I don't feel comfortable with our life together, with living in a New York suburb. I feel I'm Mr. Isabelle. I realize I need to be in control."

I moved to Cambridge, Massachusetts where Melanie was living. "Hey, Mom, why don't you move to Cambridge?" (She later moved to Portland, Oregon with her ashram—spiritual community—and later still, left it after thirteen years.) I live in walking distance of many of the stimulating activities of this university-filled town, am active in many groups—WWAM (a support group for women working alone), and a peer group of women therapists. I have many satisfactions. But one of the hardest parts about being single, many of my women friends agree, is the lack of physical contact. Lack of touch, of hugs. I often say: if each of us had a hug in the morning to start the day and a hug at night to end it, the world would be a very different place.

Finally, Bob said he realized he'd been dragging his feet on the divorce—ha! I'd begun to wonder whether the divorce agreement would have the same fate as the cigar box crystal radio (as well as our pre-nuptial contract), remaining forever unfinished. At first, he said, he had found it too hard to admit failure. I also sometimes wondered—perhaps I'm being unfair—if it didn't suit his practical convenience to be still married. A woman he was with for a time used to object when he came down to see me and stayed with me several days to work on the divorce agreement.

"I hate it when you go down to be with that woman," she'd say, by his report.

"I have to. She's my wife," he'd say. It seemed convenient to have a wife; a safety factor. He and this woman apparently had no other spoken differences. She'd had a high school education. No higher aspirations. She'd held the same secretarial job for many years. She believed Bob "knows everything in the world," by his report. Not really unlike first wife Mary. How soothing that must be.

They're no longer together. When he found his dream house, he moved.

"Did she want to marry you?" I asked.

"I don't know," he said.

He seems contented now, alone in his big new house, with four bedrooms and four acres and his beloved cats, Daisy and Tatou, and his chickens and garden and chores and projects. The house, being forty miles from most of his life-time relationships, is isolated in the snow and ice of the long winters. Up there, forty miles is a long way. But he loves the house. It's just what he wants, with its many different spaces to do his projects.

Each person chooses the way to live life. Who's to say one way is better than another?

He finally was ready to move ahead with the divorce. Yet, his travels and projects kept interfering. There was one long search to find a bedstead just like the one he and Mary shared all those "perfect" years. Once he found it, he spent many hours re-finishing it. Mary was no longer out in the cold.

With the years we've grown increasingly loving with one another—comfortable old friends with a history and an appreciation of that history and of each other.

On the #73 Bus

So . . . Listen to this, Phyllis. I answered a Personals in the *Globe.* Sounded good. He said he's tall, fit, in his fifties. Into the outdoors and cultural stuff too. Princeton graduate.

So . . . I sent off a letter with a picture . . . So . . . about a week later I get this phone call. It's this guy. He sounded intelligent. Says he's "into feelings." An architect. We talked a long time—more than half an hour. Easy to talk with. Has many interests.

He said he'd like to meet me but he's going on a consulting trip to New York for Columbia University for a week or so, and he'll phone me when he gets back.

Why are you looking at me like that?

No . . . exactly? How long ago?

Did you ever hear from him again?

This guy's name? C. H.

The very same. That swine. Can't you just picture a whole line of women, stretching back through the years . . . women he's called. He gets their hopes up and they wait weeks on end for a phone call that never comes. What a woman-hater. What an angry . . . hostile . . . vindictive . . .

Am I ever glad I told you. Well, here's my stop. See you tomorrow.

Happy Endings

Wilding caught her in his arms, and held her tight. "I bring you worship, and you answer me with scorn. But I shall prevail, and you shall come to love me in very spite of your own self . . . "

Ruth shuddered. She knew she would have to agree to the bargain. To save her brother's life she would, in one week's time, become the lawful bride of a man she hated . . .

It's a hot summer afternoon. I'm sitting in the dining room glued to a swashbuckler by Rafael Sabatini—Blackmailed Bride. I love to read. When I grow up, I want to become an actress—I'll "Hitch My Wagon to a Star." That will be a disappointment to Mama. She wants me to become a famous writer.

My brother Harris's voice comes into the dining room from the kitchen. He's telling Mama the story of a movie, scene by scene. Nothing left out. She's sitting at the kitchen counter peeling potatoes. Mama loves potatoes. She'd have them every night for dinner. Mama only wants to see or hear about movies with a happy ending. If it's a movie with Ronald Coleman, Mama wouldn't miss seeing it for the world, but Harris would tell her the story anyway. She loves a good love story.

From the dining room table where I'm sitting, (the little bedroom that my sister Lucy and I share doesn't have room for a chair or desk) the sound of Mama's laugh mixes with the sunlight streaming in through the sheer dining room curtains. The curtains billow out in the slightest breeze making the room feel cool. I can look out through them and see the tomatoes growing in Buck's garden next door. It's hot out there in the sun.

But Lucy and I were the lucky ones. Twins Mary and Bobbie had no bedroom. They slept in the same room with Mama and Papa on a lumpy pull-out olive-green studio couch that later became their bed in the upstairs hallway.

Mama bursts into laughter. She holds her arms across her breast and squinches up her face and lips. Her eyebrows go every which way. Can her hair be turning gray already? Mama is getting old. Mama, don't die.

The junkman comes along, calling out in a rasping sing-song as his cart rattles down the back alley between our back yard and Armstrong street. Mama interrupts her potato peeling and the movie story and throws open the back screen door and calls out for the junkman to wait while she runs in to get something for him. The screen door bangs shut as she hurries back for the story.

The strawberry man comes down Webster Street calling out his wares, inviting people to sample how sweet and tasty they are. Mama interrupts her potato-peeling to check out and consider the strawberries.

Today, a hobo comes along the back alley. He offers to do work for some food. Mama never turns anyone away without giving them something.

Sometimes the knife sharpener comes.

The iceman comes along with his wobbly gray truck. Like a pied piper, he's followed by the neighborhood kids squealing and scurrying for slivers of ice to suck when he cuts off a chunk of ice the size the housewife wants. She's put a card with numbers in the living room window to tell him the size of ice she wants that day. He hacks the ice off and carries it in his tongs on his padded shoulder to our icebox.

Later on, Mama will go to Puckett's, the neighborhood grocery store. That's a major event of the day. Puckett's is a long block up the street. Mr. Puckett stands behind the counter smiling with his dimple showing and exchanges neighborhood news with Mama. As she tells Mr. Puckett her list, he pulls things off the shelves with a long pole with a grabber on the end of it and stacks them on the counter. Then he adds them up with his pencil stub on the side of the brown paper bag.

She has him grind up fresh, twenty-five cents worth of hamburger for supper. She watches to make sure she's getting good meat.

"Mrs. Kohn, we have some beautiful fresh green beans today," Mr. Puckett might say.

"I'll take a half a pound," Mama might decide after considering the matter.

When one of us kids isn't with Mama to carry the bags, Mr. Puckett asks if she wants them delivered.

And Mama walks down the hill and into our unlocked cool house. I don't think we even had a key then.

The Universe Provides

I'm in line in the Cambridge HMO office, waiting to pay. In front of me is a wisp of a man, slightly hollow-chested, in his sixties.

"Do you have a good dentist here?" he asks, smiling broadly.

"I'm satisfied with the one who worked on me for the first time today," I say. "Why are you smiling?"

"I always smile," he says.

"Wait for me," I say. (A daring, uncharacteristic command. Did that really come out of me?) Here in the Northeastern U.S. many if not most people habitually go about with a pinched look rather than a big smile.

I pay my bill.

"Tell me about yourself," I say.

He says he's into meditation and the spiritual life. I wonder: a holdover from the sixties . . . or genuine? He says he has a Ph.D. in Psychology and a Ph.D. in Cultural Anthropology and has taught both at the college level . . . "sometimes in New Haven . . . not at Yale . . . in a small college."

"I have no money," he says proudly. "But I manage to do everything I want to do. I want to go to Europe now—Vienna—so I will."

"You're wearing a Harris tweed jacket," I observe.

"The Universe provides," he states.

"How do you manage? I really want to know."

"When you're clear on your goal, the Universe provides."

"But tell me how it works. It costs money to go to Vienna."

"Well," he admits slowly, almost reluctantly, as an afterthought, "I'm going to get reparations from the Viennese government; I'm a Holocaust victim" (not "survivor"?) And I stay with friends."

Ah, so! "The Universe provides" in the form of concrete fore-known reparations and the hospitality of friends. Part of me wants to puncture what feels like his phony spirituality. Another part wants to give him more of a chance. I'd like to have some male companionship in my life. I know many great women, but I lack the male presence.

"I have an article about the Holocaust that is going to be published in a Viennese periodical," he says. "If you'd like to see it, I'll send it to you," he offers.

I give him my card. (He has none.) I notice a twinge of feeling superior for which I twit myself. I'm not proud of it.

In a couple of days, the article arrives with a note saying if I'd like to talk with him some more to phone him. The article is well enough reasoned but dry, academic and poorly written. I call. We arrange a date to meet for lunch near my place the following week.

I get to the restaurant on time. He arrives a few minutes late. When he enters and sees me, he does not register that delight in connection that warms the soul. His face grows slack. I have a moment of regression to the ancient dating game: Why is he less interested today? Does he realize I am taller than he? Do I seem suddenly less interesting than before? But I look better than the day we met. I'm wearing a red silk blouse and trim white jeans.

In my mean soul (can a soul have a mean side?) I chalk up the disappointing response against him. It makes me want to move myself far from men-strangers and possible ego-bruising situations and also to exact—just possibly—a small revenge.

Still, I'm filled with questions about him and his life as I usually am. I'm often reminded of Chekhov. If he saw a person sitting alone on a park bench, he would often say, "Here's a kopeck; tell me the story of your life."

We talk about many things, including the central idea of the Celestine Prophecy—that there are no coincidences, that each meeting is for a reason—each party to it has something to learn from the other. (That doesn't mean, of course, that each party will get what's there to be learned.)

About three-quarters through lunch—he eats with enormous gusto this skinny man—I become impatient with all the focus on him. When our generation was growing up, one was supposed to ask questions of boys and men and encourage them to do all the talking.

"You haven't asked anything about me. Is there anything you're curious about?"

"If there were something you wanted me to know about yourself, I figured you'd tell me."

"Hmmm." Clearly, this man does not recognize how terrific and special and fascinating I am. It's lost on him.

We each pay for our lunch.

"I have a proposition for you," I say. "Dessert at my place—a delicious apple pie and Haagen Dasz ice cream, if you will put two large boxes in my car so I can take them to UPS."

Now, there's enthusiasm. His eyes light up. Dessert.

I feel a moment of anticipated satisfaction, of a certain maliciousness in me, for I now have a double agenda, even though he is a Holocaust survivor.

We walk the couple of blocks to my place, enter the foyer and walk up the stairs to the second floor. I open the door.

It's as though he staggers back.

"This is a huge, beautiful apartment," he says with true feeling. He keeps making "mmmmmm" sounds low in his throat as he looks around. The comic strip balloon above his head is saying, "There's money here."

My art and artifacts from around the world and the spaciousness of my condo—the big porch, the ample rooms—give the impression that I have more money than I really do. I take a malicious delight as I see the metamorphosis in this man. The spiritual aspect is down the drain. I have visions of a Walt Disney character's eyes bulging in surprise. Boing!

He puts the boxes in the car. We have hot apple pie and ice cream and hot spiced apple cider out on the porch, overlooking the garden.

"Can I do anything more for you?" he says in a very different tone now, obliging, even obsequious. The balance of power has shifted.

"No, thanks," I say, careful not to be regal.

"Well, I was planning to be in Europe six weeks, but I might come back earlier," he says, with a significant pause.

My thoughts fly back to some indelible memories of the "single scene" when I felt invisible and undesirable with the quick flick of an eye.

"Have a wonderful time," I say. Does he get it? The dismissal? No, I think not.

What power money or the appearance of it! Not very admirable of me to be so manipulative. Still . . . what the hell, am I not entitled to get back a little for some of those ego-bruising times I've experienced in the dating game? The blasted creature didn't even try to get to know me. He was, though, visibly impressed with the externals of the life I've constructed. He noticed the space. He didn't seem to pay attention to any artistry.

I had a sample of what men may routinely experience when they have the preponderance of money—and therefore power. Yes, indeed, Freud was definitely off base. It's not the penis, it's truly the power men have that women want. And are now sometimes getting. Maybe I can be forgiven for doing that little number, especially since it didn't do him any harm. He probably wasn't even conscious of the little drama we'd just enacted.

And he did get a very nice hot apple pie topped with ice cream.

So What Kept You So Long?

A Sunday afternoon poetry reading in the basement of the Middle East restaurant in Central Square, Cambridge.

The woman comes out of the winter sunlight down into the basement. The air is pungent with spices and stale breath . . . breath breathed countless times.

As the poets read, the woman notices a nice-looking older man with well-trimmed salt-and-pepper beard and neat jeans, sitting across the room. He seems to be looking right at her. He smiles broadly.

What a pleasant surprise. It's like the old days when she was young and anything exciting might happen. What a long time it's been since that film of invisibility that descends on older women here in our society has lifted.

The reading is intense. He frowns. The reading is light. He laughs. His eyes seem to seek hers. He smiles. She smiles.

Well, though she's not your standard American beauty, maybe she does still have a certain appeal. Maybe he sees her as having a piquant, interesting look—someone he'd like to get to know. And she does have a good figure. In this light he can't see her hair roots.

(It's time for a coloring. She must call for an appointment tomorrow.) She wonders if her rouge will be too much in the sunlight. She tosses about for what she might say to him when he comes over after the poetry reading ends. Maybe something like: "What kept you so long?" whimsically tossed out. He'll like that.

He may be somewhat younger than she. Oh, well, older woman/younger man has become acceptable now.

The poetry reading ends. He comes directly across the room . . . Oh, how she loves directness . . . and straight up to a young girl with yellow and green striped hair, in a layered, revealing/concealing top, a sheer see-through long flowered skirt and immense clodhopper boots. The young girl points her toe, sticks out her hip, smiles and flirts. The man smiles and smiles. Eagerly talking, they walk away.

The woman suddenly feels old, used up, unattractive. What chutzpah to think someone would see her specialness "across a crowded room" and come to her.

Back up into the sunlight. She decides she'll go have a pleasant walk along the Charles and then treat herself to a nice dinner. He doesn't know what he's missing—tossing away the Simone Signoret type richness she has to offer for the smooth thighs and un-knowingness of a clod-hoppered nymphet.

A Beginning?

At twelve-thirty on the dot he rings the bell and she buzzes him in. As he enters the apartment, she sees it momentarily as if she herself is entering for the first time. Wouldn't it be romantic, she fantasizes, if he fell in love with the creator of this universe? It's certainly welcoming and cozy, filled with light and many interesting objects artfully arranged—two huge African headdresses, a whimsical Indian sculpture, a bold drawing of a nude, a photograph of a giant sunflower, a subtle drawing of two pears and their shadows, Greek hangings, American Indian rugs.

"Any trouble finding the place?" She resorts to a standard ice-breaker opener.

"I came about a half hour early and walked around the neighborhood . . . Nice neighborhood."

"How disingenuous and refreshing," she thinks. Apparently he doesn't need to pretend nonchalance on this "first date."

He seems to be noticing everything. He looks long at the Misch Kohn print above the mantle.

"I have a collection of prints," he says.

"Whose do you especially like?"

"Matisse, Bonnard . . . "

"I'd kill to be able to render Bonnard's oranges and pinks . . . hungry? There's a little neighborhood place around the corner that does a nice lunch. And it's mercifully quiet."

"Let's go."

As they walk she notices, as she did when they met Sunday morning at the Meeting House social hour, that he has a rather stout body, but that his clothes are good and carefully coordinated—olive green corduroy pants and sweater and plaid shirt. His broad shiny face has the endearing openness and sweetness of an aging cherub.

At the restaurant, they both settle on the specialty of the house. He orders a Merlot and she has the same. She asks about his life—recently divorced, recently retired . . . three grown children . . . had been an executive . . . relocated here because of a daughter. And mirabili dictu, he asks about hers—many years in publishing, back to school for an M.S.W. A psychotherapist the last dozen-plus years. Divorced. Two grown children. Passionate about photography and art. What a treat—not to have a male monologue.

The sizing up process goes on. Each is aware of it.

He insists on paying the check. "I invited you."

After lunch he says, "I don't know how I feel about "taking out" a psychotherapist.

"Scares you, does it?" she says, thinking, how sweetly old-fashioned that expression—"taking someone out"—is but also how it constricts the new, embryonic relationship. I wish he'd see this as opening up to the possibility of a friendship and not tighten down on whether or not we'll be a pair.

She admits to herself she feels a trifle superior because she's not stuck back there in that frame.

"Well, yeh, the thought of someone analyzing everything I say."

"Well, to my kids and friends, I'm not a therapist," she says, reaching for a light touch.

Walking back to her apartment, he's quiet.

Is he afraid of saying something that would be a turn-off? Has his interest waned? Hard to tell.

Suddenly the realization hits her how "old-fashioned" she's being. She's wanting reassurance of his interest. She's already positioning her thoughts where she is waiting to see if he calls her again. What an imposter she is. Still mired in the old stuff. How about her risking?

And as in the play *Jacobowsky and the Colonel,* she reminds herself, there are always two possibilities. It was a beginning or it wasn't. If it was a beginning, there are always two possibilities . . . we might develop a friendship or we might develop a romance. What would it feel like to hug his big teddy-bear body, she wonders.

At her corner, they politely shake hands goodbye.

THE MYSTICAL UNIVERSE

I am fascinated by experiences that go beyond the material world or logical explanation, or make me reflect on the nature of life itself. Often people overlook these experiences or chalk them up to coincidence and don't pay attention to what they teach. More and more I want to allow and be connected to the mystical and mysterious in my own life. These stories present a few situations that served as a turning point for me or were critical in some other way.

Gypsy

This is a family story.

Many years ago, my father had gone to Indianapolis to bury a baby. At that time there was no cemetery in our town that would accept Jews for burial. My mother had just delivered a new baby and was in the hospital.

Waiting for the bus to carry him back to Kokomo, my father's eyes were drawn to a large luminous hand appearing out of the darkness: a Gypsy fortune teller's sign. A down-to-earth practical man, my father scoffed in his head, turned his back, moved away from the sign. But some strange tug urged him back. Finally, despite himself, he entered the doorway.

A Gypsy emerged from the back room. "Cross my palm with silver." Cursing himself for a fool, he did. "You have just buried a child," the Gypsy woman said. "Go home as fast as you can and take your wife away from where she is and get help at once. If you do not, she will be dead by morning."

The journey home seemed forever. As soon as the bus set him down in Kokomo, my father rushed to the hospital and asked to see his wife. The nurse on duty refused: "Your wife is sleeping. It's against the rules. She's fine. You may see her in the morning."

"NOW. I want to see my woman NOW." The nurse was irritated and would not budge.

My father went to get the doctor who had delivered her. He was not home. He tried several doctors in town. Finally, he found one who would help him, a black doctor. This man agreed to come to the hospital with him. The two of them ran quickly past the protesting nurse, lifted up my mother and carried her out of the hospital and home. The doctor discovered that the after-birth had been left in her body and was poisoning her. She would have been dead by morning.

Leaping Lucy

My sister Lucy used to sleepwalk when she was a child. One night, something woke up my mother and impelled her to come upstairs to the second floor bedroom that Lucy and I shared. Lucy was up on the window ledge, spreading her arms to leap. My mother ran across the room, caught her little arms and pulled her to safety. Lucy had been dreaming that someone below was going to catch her.

Typhoid and Celery Soup

When I was thirteen, I got typhoid fever. I'd gone down South to Hayti, Missouri to visit cousins and an aunt and uncle. Soon after I came back I remember suddenly feeling awful and lying down on the blue mohair sofa in the living room, too weak to do anything.

My sister Leanora was being "courted" just then by a man who was a doctor. His name was Ernest Oppenheimer and he certainly lived up to his name (spelled with an "a"—earnest). He had a pinched face and a pinched voice. Well, he examined me and his diagnosis was that I was pregnant. (I didn't even know what that meant nor did I have any idea what you had to do to get that way.)

Well, Mama had another doctor come. Yes, it was far enough back in history that doctors actually made house calls. He diagnosed my condition as typhoid fever. I was put in Mama and Papa's bedroom that was downstairs, next to the living room, so people could take care of me without going up and down the stairs. (Where did my parents sleep during this time? I have no recollection of that.)

I became weaker and weaker. I also grew to detest celery soup. The Kokomo doctor ordained that celery soup was all I could eat.

I remember once everybody was around my bed. They were crying. I remember coming up out of a deep, deep sleep—I guess now, it was a coma. I was so tired and weak, I remember—there was sort of a hummm in the room, but I don't quite know what I mean by that. I know I needed to decide whether to just let go—it was easier to do that—or to make the effort to come back. I remember deciding to come back. I opened my eyes and said, "Why is everybody crying?" And that set them off to really crying. I learned later that was the crisis and I'd passed it. The high fever broke. I would live.

I'll never forget that. How easy it would have been to just let go. I felt I had a choice. I chose to come back.

I believe, as a result of this experience, I've had less fear of death than I would otherwise; my fears have been more of illness, pain, incapacity, dying on the way to death.

I'm wondering as I say that if that is still true for me now as I approach closer to the inevitable. Or is it true, as many writers have claimed—including one of my favorite authors on the subject—Ernest Becker, author of *The Denial of Death*—that we all do fear death?

Does this apply to people in societies such as those in the East, where the belief systems include karma, life after death, reincarnation?

Recently, I had a memorable experience that felt like the way I'd like to experience my death. I was having a medical procedure. The doctor said, "Now, I'm starting the Demerol." I felt myself within about a second and a half go to sleep gently and softly. We humans do a kindness to animals putting them to sleep when it's time. Will we finally come to do it for ourselves? In traditional Eskimo societies older Eskimos were put out on an ice floe or in an igloo. Once the person died, the igloo was destroyed or allowed to melt. It was never used again.

If we thought our life would not be dragged out by our technological capabilities past the point where we wanted such measures, if we could have a say in when this life is finished for us—when the bad stuff over balances the good—would we not live better lives along the way, with more tranquility, knowing we could come to the end with dignity?

. . . While I Am in This Life . . .

He was a young and beautiful man, in a gold brocaded robe. His hair was black and curly, full of life. He lay on a wooden pyre, on the steps leading down to the river, a branch of the holy Ganges. A young woman (his wife? his sister?) and an older woman (his mother? his mother-in-law?) huddled over him, wailing, holding their robes in front of their eyes while an official carried on the rituals, preparing him for the fire. Then he covered the young man with straw and lit the fire. The flames rose high. The two women, bent with grief, were led away on the arms of family members. The young man's feet were still uncovered as the fire crackled and burned, the flames rising higher. Life went on around the burning pyre. Merchants hawked their wares—bibelots, jewelry, colorful leis of flowers for offerings to the gods.

The young man's feet looked so vulnerable as the flames leapt higher.

A dog defecated into the river. A pack of monkeys scampered about, scratching themselves and screeching merrily.

An old man clad in a loincloth and a bright orange turban sat in the lotus position, meditating.

Women did their laundry . . . in the river.

Women washed their hair . . . in the river.

Men and women drank . . . from the river.

A passerby was heard to say, ". . . while I am in this life . . ."